my **revision** notes

OCR Cambridge Nationals

CREATIVE iMEDIA L1/2 RO81 PRE-PRODUCTION SKILLS AND R082 CREATING DIGITAL GRAPHICS

Kevin Wells

HODDER
EDUCATION
AN HACHETTE UK COMPANY

The Publishers would like to thank the following for permission to reproduce copyright material:

Adobe product screenshots reprinted with permission from Adobe Systems Incorporated.

Photo credits

t = **top.** *b* = **bottom,** *l* = **left,** *c* = **centre,** *r* = **right**

p. 1 © Kevin Wells; **p. 3** © Kevin Wells; **p. 4** © James Quine / Alamy Stock Photo; **p. 8** © Couperfield – Fotolia; **p. 10** © Pens Forms / Alamy Stock Photo; **p. 13** *t* © Zoonar GmbH / Alamy Stock Photo, *b* © scanrail /123RF; **p. 15** © Sergey Jarochkin/123RF; **p. 17** © Illustration Works / Alamy Stock Photo; **p. 19** © Illia Uriadnikov/123RF; **p. 20** © zerbor/123RF; **p. 22** © Cultura RM / Alamy Stock Photo; **p. 23** © Kevin Wells; **p. 24** © Kevin Wells; **p. 25** © Kevin Wells; **p.** *t* **27** © Kristina Afanasyeva /123RF, *b* © Kevin Wells; **p. 28** © rashpil / Alamy Stock Photo; **p. 29** © gmast3r /123RF; **p. 30** © Kevin Wells; **p. 31** © Aydin Buyuktas / Alamy Stock Photo; **p. 33** © Eye Risk / Alamy Stock Photo; **p. 34** © Sergii Lysenkov / Alamy Stock Photo; **p. 39** © VisitBritain/Britain on View/VisitBritain/Getty Images; **p. 40** © Kevin Wells; **p. 41** *l* © Kevin Wells, *r* © Kevin Wells; **p. 43** © Kevin Wells; **p. 47** © Kevin Wells; **p. 48** © Kevin Wells; **p. 49** © Yuri_Arcurs/E+/Getty Images; **p. 50** *t* © Kevin Wells, *b* © Kevin Wells; **p. 53** © Kevin Wells; **p. 70** © Kevin Wells; **p. 71** © Kevin Wells; **p. 72** © Kevin Wells; **p. 73** © Kevin Wells; **p. 74** © Kevin Wells; **p. 77** © Kevin Wells

Every effort has been made to trace all copyright holders, but if any have been inadvertently overlooked the Publishers will be pleased to make the necessary arrangements at the first opportunity.

Although every effort has been made to ensure that website addresses are correct at time of going to press, Hodder Education cannot be held responsible for the content of any website mentioned in this book. It is sometimes possible to find a relocated web page by typing in the address of the home page for a website in the URL window of your browser.

Hachette UK's policy is to use papers that are natural, renewable and recyclable products and made from wood grown in sustainable forests. The logging and manufacturing processes are expected to conform to the environmental regulations of the country of origin.

Orders: please contact Bookpoint Ltd, 130 Milton Park, Abingdon, Oxon OX14 4SB.

Telephone: +44 (0)1235 827720. Fax: +44 (0)1235 400454. Lines are open 9.00a.m.–5.00p.m., Monday to Saturday, with a 24-hour message answering service. Visit our website at www.hoddereducation.co.uk

© Kevin Wells 2017

First published in 2017 by

Hodder Education,

An Hachette UK Company

Carmelite House

50 Victoria Embankment

London EC4Y 0DZ

Impression number 10 9 8 7 6 5

Year 2021 2020 2019 2018

Cover photo © iStock/Getty Images/Thinkstock

Typeset in Bembo Std Regular, 11/13 pt by Aptara, Inc.

Printed in Spain

A catalogue record for this title is available from the British Library

ISBN 978 1471 886683

Features to help you succeed

Think about it

These features are a prompt for you to pause your revision reading. They will help to develop your understanding by considering what would happen in a given situation.

Check your understanding

These activities will help you to understand each topic in an interactive way.

Now test yourself

These short, knowledge-based questions provide the first step in testing your learning. Answers are on p. 35 and 78–9.

Exam tips

Expert tips are given throughout the book to help you polish your exam technique in order to maximise your marks in the exam.

Exam practice

Practice exam questions are provided for each topic. Use them to consolidate your revision and practise your exam skills. Answers are on pp. 36–7.

Key words

Clear, concise definitions of essential key terms are provided where they first appear.

Get the most from this book

Everyone has to decide his or her own revision strategy, but it is essential to review your work, learn it and test your understanding. These Revision Notes will help you to do that in a planned way, topic by topic. Use this book as the cornerstone of your revision and don't hesitate to write in it – personalise your notes and check your progress by ticking off each section as you revise.

Tick to track your progress

Use the revision planner on pages v and vi to plan your revision, topic by topic. Tick each box when you have:

- revised and understood a topic
- tested yourself
- practised the exam questions and checked your answers at the back of the book.

You can also keep track of your revision by ticking off each topic heading in the book. You may find it helpful to add your own notes as you work through each topic.

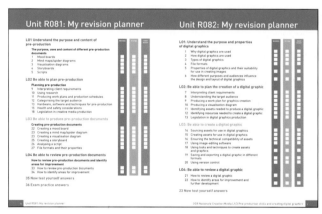

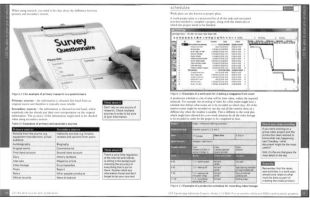

Introduction – how to use this book

The Cambridge Nationals in Creative iMedia qualification comprises 12 different subject units. Each unit requires 30 hours of study time, which includes the time needed for the final assignment. There are three different sizes of qualifications:

Award in Creative iMedia: Complete **two** units, including the examined unit R081 (pre-production) and the mandatory R082 (digital graphics).

Certificate in Creative iMedia: Complete **four** units, including the examined unit R081, the mandatory R082 and two additional units from R083 to R092.

Diploma in Creative iMedia: Complete **eight** units, including the examined unit R081, the mandatory R082 and six additional units from R083 to R092.

This book is separated into two parts that cover the two mandatory units. The first part is for the examined R081 unit on pre-production. For this you can work through the content as a revision guide, checking your progress and understanding along the way. You should then be in a position to work through some practice papers, which your teacher may provide before your final examination in January or June. The second part is for the R082 coursework unit on creating digital graphics. The content of this part can be used alongside your learning before starting on your final assignment.

Unit R081: My revision planner

LO1 Understand the purpose and content of pre-production

		REVISED	TESTED	EXAM READY

The purpose, uses and content of different pre-production documents

1   Mood boards
2   Mind maps/spider diagrams
3   Visualisation diagrams
4   Storyboards
5   Scripts

LO2 Be able to plan pre-production

Planning pre-production

9   Interpreting client requirements
10   Using research
11   Producing work plans and production schedules
12   Categorising the target audience
13   Hardware, software and techniques for pre-production
15   Health and safety considerations
18   Legislation in creative media production

LO3 Be able to produce pre-production documents

Creating pre-production documents

22   Creating a mood board
23   Creating a mind map/spider diagram
23   Creating a visualisation diagram
25   Creating a storyboard
26   Analysing a script
27   File formats and their properties

LO4 Be able to review pre-production documents

How to review pre-production documents and identify areas for improvement

33   How to review pre-production documents
34   How to identify areas for improvement

35 Now test yourself answers

36 Exam practice answers

Unit R082: My learning planner

LO1: Understand the purpose and properties of digital graphics

		LEARNED	TESTED	ASSIGNMENT READY
40	Why digital graphics are used	☐	☐	☐
40	How digital graphics are used	☐	☐	☐
41	Types of digital graphics	☐	☐	☐
42	File formats	☐	☐	☐
42	Properties of digital graphics and their suitability for use in creating images	☐	☐	☐
43	How different purposes and audiences influence the design and layout of digital graphics	☐	☐	☐

LO2: Be able to plan the creation of a digital graphic

46	Interpreting client requirements	☐	☐	☐
46	Understanding the target audience	☐	☐	☐
47	Producing a work plan for graphics creation	☐	☐	☐
48	Producing a visualisation diagram	☐	☐	☐
48	Identifying assets needed to produce a digital graphic	☐	☐	☐
49	Identifying resources needed to create a digital graphic	☐	☐	☐
52	Legislation in digital graphics production	☐	☐	☐

LO3: Be able to create a digital graphic

55	Sourcing assets for use in digital graphics	☐	☐	☐
56	Creating assets for use in digital graphics	☐	☐	☐
56	Ensuring the technical compatibility of assets	☐	☐	☐
56	Using image-editing software	☐	☐	☐
61	Using tools and techniques to create assets and graphics	☐	☐	☐
74	Saving and exporting a digital graphic in different formats	☐	☐	☐
75	Using version control	☐	☐	☐

LO4: Be able to review a digital graphic

76	How to review a digital graphic	☐	☐	☐
76	How to identify areas for improvement and further development	☐	☐	☐

78 Now test yourself answers

Introduction to Unit R081 Pre-Production Skills

Pre-production is an important step in the planning for any creative media project. It enables you to create the right product in a suitable style so that it will meet the client's requirements and will satisfy them. The knowledge and skills developed in this core unit will help you in all of the additional coursework units.

Preparing for the exam

As part of this unit, you will learn about the importance of planning and pre-production when being involved with creative media projects. In this revision guide we will review the key points to prepare you for the exam. You can use this guide as a workbook with opportunities to revise and then test what you have learned. The three main areas covered by the exam are:

- knowledge of pre-production concepts, techniques and planning considerations
- skills in creating and reviewing the different types of pre-production documents
- understanding of pre-production concepts. You will be able to evidence your understanding by applying your knowledge to a specific scenario that is found in the exam paper.

Exam command words

Create – you need to actually draw the answer.

Describe – your answer must include some characteristics in addition to stating what it is. You could use words to express an overall concept, idea or need so that it is clear for the reader/listener.

Discuss – your answer must give both sides of the argument.

Evaluate – you must apply your knowledge and understanding in order to arrive at an overall judgement that takes into account a number of different factors.

Explain – your answer must include comments on the purposes and reasons for your statement. An easy way to think of this is to state what and why!

Identify – your answer just states what it is.

Justify – you must give reasons to support your choice or statement.

Exam key words

Improvements – a description of what is needed to make the product better.

Items – objects that are on a document.

Purpose – what is it used for. The reason.

Strengths – the best parts about something, i.e. what works really well.

Weaknesses – the worst parts or those that need to be better.

How to use this book

Exam technique is about answering the question and not just writing about something that you know. Marks are only given where it shows that you understand what is being asked. Some questions will have an applied context. Your answer must relate to this, so include a reference or connection to the scenario as part of your answer. An applied context means it is similar to what it would be like in a real-world scenario when creating digital media. Bear in mind that it is only your first answer(s) that will support any marks – multiple attempts won't be given marks even if the right answer is at the end.

> **Exam tip**
>
> The number of dotted lines in the answer space are a clue as to how much you should write. For example, a question that has 3 marks available would typically have 3 answer lines.

Purpose What is it used for – the reason.

Assets Images, logos and text information that are used as part of the digital graphic.

Resources The equipment that you will use to create the digital graphics, including both the hardware and software.

Properties The number of pixels, dpi resolution and file format of the digital graphics.

Strengths The best parts about something, i.e. what works really well.

Weaknesses The worst parts about something or those that need to be better.

Improvements A description of what is needed to make the product better.

L01 Understand the purpose and content of pre-production

The purpose, uses and content of different pre-production documents

Mood boards

A mood board is a collection of sample materials and products. It can be either a physical mood board or a digital mood board.

A physical mood board is, for example, created on a notice board or large piece of paper/card using pictures and samples that are fixed to it.

A digital mood board is, for example, created in any software application that supports multiple images, graphics, text and other content.

Figure 1.1 Example of a mood board

Purpose of a mood board
- To assist the generation of ideas by collecting a wide range of material that will give a 'feel' for what is needed.
- To stimulate creativity and innovative approaches.

Uses of a mood board
- For any creative media project as a starting point.
- To collect samples, materials and a range of relevant content.
- As a constant reminder of possible styles.

Note that the use of a mood board is *not* to show what a product will look like.

> **Exam tip**
>
> Remember that the *purpose* = what it is going to be used for.

Content of a mood board

- Images – from anything that is relevant or related, such as existing similar products, photographs, logos, screenshots from films, advertisements, posters.
- Colours – especially those that fit the brief or have been used before in a similar product.
- Text, key words, fonts and styles.
- Textures, fabrics and other materials.
- For a digital mood board – potentially sounds and video clips.

Mind maps/spider diagrams

A mind map or spider diagram is a way of organising thoughts and ideas. It is based around a central theme (or **node**) and has **branches** off for the different aspects using **sub-nodes**.

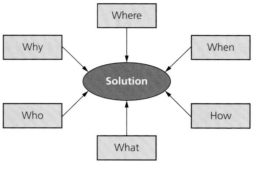

> **Node** A point on the mind map that has some information or an idea.
>
> **Sub-node** A point that also has information or an idea but must be related to the node that it is connected to.
>
> **Branch** A line that joins the node to the sub-node.

Figure 1.2 **Example of the content for a mind map or spider diagram**

Purpose of a mind map/spider diagram

- To quickly generate outline ideas.
- To develop and show links between different thoughts, aspects and processes of a project.

Uses of a mind map/spider diagram

- To show the development and options for ideas in any project.
- To show the connections and links between different parts of the project.

Content of a mind map/spider diagram

- Central node with the main theme.
- Sub-nodes with interconnecting lines or branches for the different parts.
- Text at each sub-node for key points, ideas, activities, requirements etc.
- Images can also be used on sub-nodes.

Check your understanding

Label each part of the diagram using the words provided.

Words/phrases to use:
- Node
- Sub-node
- Branch
- Main theme or idea.

This is a rough drawing or sketch of what the final static image product is intended to look like. Typically, it is hand drawn, but good art skills are not essential – it is the concept, layout and content of the product that is being illustrated. A static or still image is one that does not move, so something like a magazine advert, DVD cover or website page would be good examples, although don't use these for anything that has a timeline, such as a video.

Figure 1.3 Example of a visualisation diagram

Purpose of a visualisation diagram

● To plan the layout of a static or still image in a visual manner.
● To show how a finished item might look.

Uses of a visualisation diagram

● To give to a client or production team to show what the intended product will look like, for example:
  ○ CD/DVD/Blu-ray™ cover
  ○ poster, e.g. for a film, event or advertisement
  ○ game scene or display screen, e.g. for the game environment or game menus
  ○ comic book page layout
  ○ web page/multimedia page layout
  ○ magazine front cover or advertisement for use on an inside page.

Content of a visualisation diagram

● Multiple images and graphics showing their size and position.
● Colours and colour schemes.
● Position and style of text.
● Fonts to be used.
● **Annotations** to provide more detail where needed.

Think about it

A graphic designer needs to create something that the client will be happy with so they need to be given enough information on content and layout to do this – otherwise the work could be unsuitable and the client might hire another designer instead.

Annotations Your own thoughts, notes and comments that help to show your thinking. Used on visualisation diagrams and other draft pre-production documents.

Storyboards

REVISED

A storyboard is used to illustrate a sequence of moving images, and has a flow of scenes that follow a timeline. This is different to a visualisation diagram, which would only be for a single static scene.

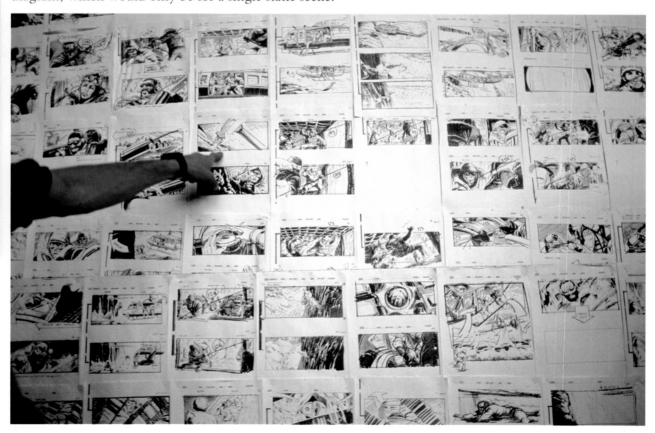

Figure 1.4 Example of a storyboard

Purpose of a storyboard

- To provide a visual representation of how a media project will look along a timeline.
- To provide a graphical illustration of what a sequence of movements will look like.
- To provide guidance on what scenes to film or create.
- To provide guidance on how to edit the scenes into a story.

Uses of a storyboard

- Any project where movement or a sequence is required, especially along a timeline, for example:
  - video projects
  - digital animation
  - comic books to illustrate the story
  - computer games, i.e. to illustrate the game flow, narrative or story
  - multimedia products, i.e. to illustrate the sequence between scenes.

Content of a storyboard

- Images, i.e. for the content of each scene
- Locations
- Camera shot types and angles
- Camera movement
- Shot length and timings
- Lighting
- Sound.

> **Check your understanding**
>
> State how and why a client and a video editor would use a storyboard.
>
> *Hint: Think about why they want to see it.*

Scripts

A script is a piece of written work that can be for a movie, audio, audio-visual product or screenplay. It is often the starting point for any of these products and includes information about the media product in a style and format that follows some layout conventions. It is often used by a number of different people involved in the actual production, who will analyse the script and break it down into sections with information that is needed.

```
                SCRIPT - THE GAMING OFFICE
EXT. GAME DEVELOPER CAR PARK - DAY
It's early morning. Peter and Mary are walking into the
office.

                PETER
        Hi Mary! Busy day today?


                MARY
        Oh hi, Peter! Yes - I need to fully
        test Level 6 of the new game by the
        end of the day.


                PETER
        I take it that's a lot to do then? Do
        you need any help with it?


                MARY
        Well, if you want to volunteer, that
        would be great, but I know you have a
        lot to do as well. Paul will be working
        with me so I'm hoping it will be fine.
```

Figure 1.5 Example of a script

Purpose of a script

- To identify the location where the action takes place.
- To identify who will be in the scene, e.g. actors, **narrators**.
- To provide stage directions for actors and production crew.
- To provide **dialogue** (i.e. speech) for actors and other characters.

Uses of a script

- Any moving product with dialogue (spoken words), actions and a timeline, for example:
  - video products, e.g. advertisements, films
  - audio products, e.g. advertisements, jingles, radio play
  - animation products, e.g. short films
  - computer game with a short story-telling scene or interaction between game characters.

Content of a script

- Set or locations where the action takes place, e.g. INT. (Interior) and EXT. (Exterior)
- Scene descriptions
- Scene/stage directions, i.e. what happens in the scene
- Camera shot types
- Camera movement
- Sounds and sound effects
- Names of actors/characters
- Dialogue, i.e. speech and how it is spoken.

The format and layout of a script should follow some conventions. For example, the location, camera shot and directions all start in the left-hand margin but names of actors and what they say are indented across the page. This makes it easier and quicker to scan and follow.

Narrator A person that tells the story who is not part of, or seen, in any action. Typically found in a screenplay or audio-visual product.

Dialogue The combination of what is spoken by a character in the script together with how they say it, that is, identifying any emotion, facial expressions etc.

Voiceover The words spoken by an unseen person to accompany an audio or audio-visual product. Often used in radio adverts and jingles.

Check your understanding

How might the following people use a script and what key information would they look for?
- Client
- Actor
- Camera operator
- Stage manager or set director
- Sound editor

Exam tip

Some questions will be looking for an answer that is in context for the question and scenario. That means a vague or generic answer about the purpose of a storyboard will not get full marks. If the question makes reference to a particular context or project, then phrase your answer in a way that relates to this. Something like: 'I would use ... for ...'.

Now test yourself

1 Depending on what type of media product is being created, the type of pre-production document will vary. Tick which type of pre-production document could be used for the media products listed in the table.

Media product:	Mood board	Mind map	Visualisation	Storyboard	Script
Poster for music event					
CD or DVD cover					
2D/3D character					
Comic book					
Company website					
Animated short film					
Radio jingle					
Video advertisement					
Computer game					

2 Which pre-production documents would be suitable if the media product has a timeline?

3 What might you see on a script that is not shown on a storyboard?

4 If you wanted to generate some ideas for a new computer game, what sort of pre-production document might you start with?

5 What two types of pre-production document are not needed when planning a static image such as the front cover for a magazine?

6 If you wanted to know how many actors are needed for a video trailer, what pre-production document would you ask to see?

7 If you wanted to show your client an idea for the layout of a new website home page, what type of pre-production document would you use?

Exam practice

Music Snackbox is a new music magazine that is due to launch in February. The magazine will include reviews of the latest releases and live performances from a wide variety of musical genres. The magazine is targeted at people of all genders between the ages of 15 and 60 who are interested in music. *Music Snackbox* will be published in both digital and printed format so that it can be read by as wide a range of people as possible. The digital version can also be updated daily, whilst the paper version will be published every Thursday.

1 You have been asked to create the style and look for the *Music Snackbox* magazine.
   (a) Identify the most suitable pre-production document that can be used to show your ideas. [1]
   (b) Explain why this is the most suitable pre-production document to use for showing your ideas for the new magazine's style and look. [3]

2 You have been asked to create a visualisation diagram for the front screen of issue one of the digital version of *Music Snackbox*. Identify three items that could be included on the visualisation diagram. [3]

Exam tip

'Because' is a very useful word when answering a question that asks you to explain something and using it might mean that you could earn extra marks. Your answer to an 'explain' question should state 'what' and 'why'. Something like: 'I would use ... because ...'.

LO2 Be able to plan pre-production

Planning pre-production

Planning and pre-production for any media project begins with a description of what is needed. This might come from a set of **client** requirements, a commission or written specification. Before starting work on this, you will need to review and interpret these project or product requirements. This is where you have a chance to demonstrate your own creative thoughts and ideas.

Note that all of this section for LO2 is about *planning* before actually creating any pre-production documents. It involves interpreting what is needed by the client, using research, developing work plans, health and safety, categorising the audience, hardware and software and legislation.

> **Client** The person, organisation or company that you are producing the work for.

Figure 2.1 Agreeing client requirements

Interpreting client requirements

Whether you are creating something for yourself or for a client, your project will have a set of client requirements (also known as a brief or specification). If it's something for yourself, then you are the client. For this course, you will always be producing something for someone else. It is important to meet the client requirements, otherwise your work will not be fit for purpose.

Purpose of client requirements

- To provide the media developer with outline information and any constraints for the project, such as timescale.
- A clear statement of what is to be produced, even though this may not explain how.
- To identify the intention for the product and perhaps what is hoped to be achieved.

Think about it

Think about who will be *using* the list of client requirements. That will help you to understand the reason or purpose for producing them.

Content of client requirements

- Statement of what media product is needed
- The purpose of that media product
- Who the **target audience** will be
- An indication of the content for the media product
- Timescale for when the product will be needed
- Constraints and restrictions
- Details of any **house style** to make sure the product is consistent with the organisation's own branding and recognised style.

It is quite likely that the initial set of client requirements will not answer everything. This is where you might need to discuss the details with the client further and request a more detailed brief.

Think about it

If a client just said they wanted to advertise their products, you wouldn't really know where to start. Information is needed to decide what sort of media product is wanted, such as a poster or video. The client might have some thoughts about what they want, but your own ideas on how to achieve that will be the basis of your own interpretation.

Target audience This is usually the final viewer or consumer of the product that is to be created. However, it can also be the person who will be the user of the pre-production document.

House style Many organisations will have an established brand identity that includes set colour schemes, design styles, fonts and logos. It is likely that any new creative media product will have to follow the organisation's own house style so that it is consistent and recognisable.

Using research

When using research, you need to be clear about the difference between primary and secondary sources.

Figure 2.2 An example of primary research is a questionnaire

Primary sources – the information is obtained first hand from an original source and therefore is typically more reliable.

Secondary sources – the information is obtained second hand, where somebody else has already put their own interpretation on the original information. The accuracy of the information might need to be checked when using secondary sources.

Table 2.1 Examples of primary and secondary sources

Primary sources	Secondary sources
Directly from the source, e.g. equipment manufacturer, actual audience	Indirectly sourced, e.g. forums, reviews and opinions from users
Autobiography	Biography
Original works	Commentaries
First-hand account	Second-hand account
Diary	History textbook
Interview	Magazine article
Video footage	Encyclopaedias
Photo	Report
Relics	Other people's products
Official records	News broadcast

Think about it

Don't rely on one source of research. Check multiple sources in order to be sure of your information.

Think about it

There is very little regulation of the internet and nobody is sitting in the background checking the accuracy of everything that is put on there. Double check any information found and don't forget to list your sources!

Producing work plans and production schedules

Work plans are also known as project plans.

A work/project plan is a structured list of all the tasks and associated activities needed to complete a project, along with the timescales in which the project needs to be finished.

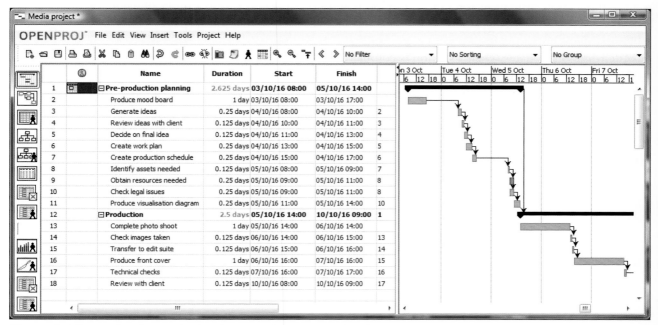

Figure 2.3 Example of a work plan for creating a magazine front cover

A production schedule is a list of what will be done when, within the required timescale. For example, the recording of video for a film trailer might have a schedule that defines what scenes are to be recorded on which days. All of the interior scenes might be recorded on one day and all the exterior shots on a different day when the weather is suitable. This is different to the work plan which might have allowed for a two-week duration for all the video footage to be recorded in order for the project to be completed in time.

Project	Video – Adventure trekking promotion		
Production task	Outdoor scenes 4, 5, 6, and 7		
Date	1st October	**Start time**	6.30 a.m.
Main location	Helvellyn, Lake District		
People needed	Cast: Richard (Climber 1) Jackie (Climber 2)	Crew: Camera operator Sound recorder	Other: Director
Time	Scene	Characters/actors	Location
6.30	1.1 – packing gear	Richard Jackie	Car park
6.45	1.2 – setting off	Richard Jackie	Approaching Helvellyn on waymarked path
7.30	1.3 – viewing the mountain range	Richard Jackie	Grid ref 349149 Looking east
11.00	1.4 – scrambling above Red Tarn	Richard	Striding Edge

Figure 2.4 Example of a production schedule for recording video footage

Check your understanding

If you were working on a group video project and the production team wanted to know what was happening next Tuesday – what document might be the most useful?

Hint: It's the one that gives the most detail on the day.

Exam tip

Remember that the tasks and activities in a work plan should only relate to what must be done as part of creating the media product.

Purpose of a work plan

- To provide a timescale for the overall project to be completed.
- To map out against time all the different aspects of the project.

Content of a work plan

- Tasks – the different stages or main sections of the overall project.
- Activities – a series of things to do in order to complete a task.
- Durations – the amount of time that a task or activity is expected to take.
- Timescales – how long the overall project will take to complete.
- Milestones – key dates when a section is completed.
- Deadlines – a date when something must be completed by.
- Resources – what is needed to do the tasks and activities.
- Contingencies – 'what if' scenarios, back-up plans such as extra time or alternative ways to do things.

Uses of a work plan

- Any media product, for example:
  - comic book
  - interactive multimedia product, e.g. a website
  - audio advertisement, e.g. for radio broadcast
  - video, e.g. film trailer
  - digital animation
  - photographic shoot
  - computer game.

> **Work flow** This is the order that the activities will be completed in but can also be the sequence within a software application between importing assets and exporting the final output.

> **Check your understanding**
>
> Imagine the media product is a video advertisement for a mobile phone; make a list of who might need or want to use the work plan.
>
> *Hint: Who is involved with any part of the production?*

Categorising the target audience

REVISED

The expectations, needs and requirements of the target audience must always be considered so that the media product can be successful. Knowing how to categorise the audience for a product is vital and this can be done in several ways:

- Age – be clear about the age group. This can be a range such as 6–12, 12–18, 18–40, 40+.
- Gender – male and female, but also consider trans-gender.
- Location – the main groups are local, national and international. The promotion of a media product might target one of these groups more than others; think about a small local music event compared with a national music festival.
- Ethnicity – we live in a multi-cultural society and ethnic groups are found on a local as well as national and international level. Ethnic groups can be defined as a group of people that have a common background or culture, whether through race, religion or language.

> **Think about it**
>
> If identifying an audience by age, don't just use the term 'old people'. Somebody who is 16 might think 25 is 'old' but if you're 40, then 25 is 'young'. Don't describe an audience using personal judgements or opinions with any category, since this might be seen as discrimination or prejudice at times.

Figure 2.5 Identifying your target audience

Exam tip

Make sure you can give examples for each of the categories of a target audience.

Hardware, software and techniques for pre-production

REVISED

In this unit, the terms **hardware** and **software** relate to their use in creating pre-production documents rather than the final products.

Hardware

The devices and equipment that could be used to create or digitise pre-production documents are, for example:

- a computer system, e.g. PC (desktop or laptop), Mac® but also tablets such as an iPad®
- computer peripherals, e.g. keyboard, mouse, track pad, graphics tablet, display monitor, microphone, speakers
- imaging devices, e.g. digital camera, scanner
- other equipment, e.g. pens, pencils, paper (since some pre-production documents could be drawn by hand).

Hardware The equipment used.

Software Programs or applications used to create pre-production documents (which is different to the software used for reports or web research).

Resources covers both hardware, software and people.

Think about it

Digitising any form of pre-production document is a great way to keep back-ups. At least then, it isn't such a big problem if a paper-based version goes missing, since you always have a copy to work from.

Exam tip

Make sure you know the difference between *identifying* and *describing* any resources that could be used. These key terms are explained on page vi.

Figure 2.6 Computer hardware

Software

There are many different types of application which could be used to create or digitise pre-production documents and each can be used for different purposes.

- Image editing or desktop publishing: Adobe Photoshop®, Illustrator®, Serif Drawplus/Affinity Designer®, Pixelmator, Microsoft Publisher®.
  - Used to create a digital mood board, visualisation diagram or storyboard.
- Word processing: Microsoft Word®, Apple Pages®.
  - Used to create a visualisation diagram, storyboard or edit a script.
- Presentation software: Microsoft PowerPoint®, Apple Keynote®.
  - Used to create a visualisation diagram or mood board.
- Web browser: Internet Explorer®, Safari®, Firefox®, Chrome™.
  - Used to obtain content for a mood board, or for online applications such as mind maps.
- Dedicated software applications: for example 'Freemind' for mind maps, 'Storyboard That™' or Toon Boom Storyboard™.

Note that a spreadsheet application would not typically be used to create any of the main pre-production documents, although it would have a use in planning, such as to create work plans or to log the use of assets.

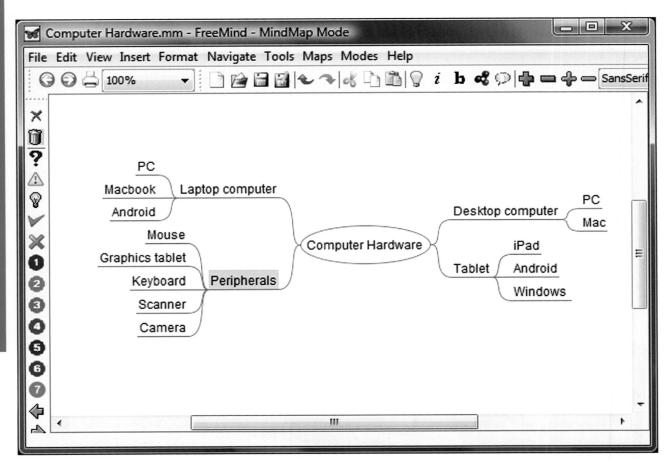

Figure 2.7 Using apps on a tablet to create pre-production documents

Techniques for pre-production documents

There are two techniques used in making pre-production documents: creating and **digitising**.

Creating is where you use the hardware devices to create the original pre-production document in a digital or electronic format. You then save work using a suitable file name and file format.

Digitising is where you create the pre-production by hand, such as a physical mood board with pictures placed on it. Any of the pre-production documents for this unit could be created by hand, but you may then want to digitise these into an electronic format that could be distributed or stored. Methods of digitising these would include:
- photographing the work, such as for a mood board or mind map
- scanning the work, such as for a visualisation diagram or storyboard.

> **Digitising** means making a digital copy that can be stored and distributed electronically.

> **Think about it**
>
> Scanning is a good option for A4 documents but a digital camera is a quick way for anything much larger. Think about what you could do with photographs, video clips and even sound recordings.

> **Check your understanding**
>
> Hardware can be used both to create and digitise pre-production documents.
>
> Think about the difference between these activities. If you have a physical mood board in the form of a pin board with pictures and notes on it, how would you digitise it?
>
> *Hint: It's quite large and you need a digital copy that you can put on a computer.*
>
> How would you create the following?
>
> | Pre-production document | Method |
> | --- | --- |
> | Mood board made up of a wide range of pictures taken from magazines | |
> | A mind map that can be displayed at all times so that people can add their own comments and ideas | |
>
> How would you digitise the following?
>
> | Pre-production document | Method |
> | --- | --- |
> | Large mood board created on an A1-sized pin board | |
> | A storyboard on several sheets of A4 paper | |

> **Exam tip**
>
> Make sure you understand the difference between creating something original in a digital format and digitising what has already been created.

Health and safety considerations

REVISED ☐

Recce

A **recce** is a visit to a specific location that will be used for recording purposes, e.g. filming, audio recording or photography. The purpose is to check access, see what is there, identify the best positions and assess environmental considerations.

The recce report may include notes on:
- location and how to get there
- access – a check that it's suitable
- lighting
- health and safety issues
- availability of power, e.g. electricity
- environmental considerations, e.g. background noise, people
- any other potential issues that may arise.

Location recce			
Completed by: _____		Date: _____	
Location	Used for	Potential issues	Actions required

Figure 2.8 Example of a recce form

Risk assessment

In general, this needs to be completed for any media project but the risks will vary depending on what activities you need to complete and whether any recording of material will be done outside. A risk assessment may be completed at the same time as a location recce. The process of completing a risk assessment is:
- identify the hazards and dangers
- decide who might be harmed and how
- evaluate the risks and decide on precautions to be taken
- record your findings and implement them
- review your assessment and update if necessary.

Figure 2.9 Risk assessment processes

Risk assessments can be completed using a standard form or template. These must be stored to cover you and any organisation that you work for in case of claims against you at a later date.

> **Recce** is the abbreviation for 'reconnaissance' and is a term that is commonly used in media projects.

> **Check your understanding**
>
> Let's say that you have an assignment to photograph a local carnival. You have been given a route and date but don't really know what to expect. What might you want to check as part of a recce?
>
> *Hint: Where will you take the photographs from?*

> **Think about it**
>
> What would happen if you did not complete a risk assessment and an accident happened?
> Who would be accountable – the organisation or you?
> What would you have in your defence?

Safe working practices

You should be aware of the safety procedures for the following areas of working practice.

Using computers

The main thing when using computers for any length of time is to make sure that you are not straining any part of your body. Examples include eyes, arms, back and shoulders, since long periods of sitting at a computer in a poor position can cause repetitive strain injury (RSI). Considerations must include:

● chair height – to make sure your eyes are at the same height as the display
● seating position – to maintain a good posture and keep your back straight
● distance from screen to eyes – so that you can read the text easily and not strain your eyes
● keyboards/mice – make sure they are in a comfortable and natural position for your hands to reach.

Figure 2.10 Using a computer safely

Working at heights

The main things to consider when working at heights are the risks of falling or dropping anything. Safety barriers are needed for people working above ground level since they might be distracted if they needed to look through a viewfinder. You would also need to consider the safety of people below and that of equipment which is breakable if dropped. Typical applications would be high platforms to get a good viewpoint for:

● filming using video cameras
● photography using digital still cameras.

Working with electricity

This covers the use of electrical cables (both high and low voltage) together with consideration of the environment, both indoor and outdoor. Risk factors include the following:

● cable safety on the ground – loose cables can become trip hazards, causing people to fall and could potentially damage the equipment that cables are connected to
● location – if outdoors, are there any damp/wet conditions or is there any chance of rain?

Working with heavy equipment

Some equipment used in creative media production can be heavy, especially when stored in a transit case. This might need two people to lift the equipment into position, whether into a vehicle or on location. Typical risk factors include:

- lifting – using the correct handling techniques to prevent back injury
- moving – being in a stable position and avoiding twisting
- setting up – you may need two people, one to hold the camera or lights in position while the other tightens the stand or tripod mount.

Legislation in creative media production

There are several areas of legislation that you need to know about:
- use of copyrighted material and intellectual property
- certification and classification
- data protection
- privacy and defamation.

Table 2.2 Symbols used to protect work, ideas and organisations

Symbol	©	TM	®
Meaning	Copyright	Trademark	Registered

Copyright and intellectual property

The general rule is that pretty much everything will have some form of copyright protection but it might not be clear who owns it or how rigidly the protection will be enforced. Anything that has been published is likely to have copyright protection.

The term 'published' covers:
- photographs, images and graphics in books, magazines and on the internet
- music on CD, DVD, downloaded from iTunes or equivalent, streamed on Spotify or equivalent
- movies on DVD, Blu-ray disc, TV, Netflix or similar.

In fact, *all* content on the internet is likely to be protected by copyright unless it specifically says it isn't (such as freeware).

To use published resources, you must:
- contact the owner
- ask for permission to use it
- be prepared to pay a fee.

Some people are happy for their products and work to be used by others but still want to have some protection and recognition. In the UK, copyright does not have to be registered – it is automatic and belongs to the author or creator unless transferred by written agreement.

You cannot get around copyright by creating your own version of somebody else's work, e.g. by tracing around it or photographing it. Copyright protection is there to prevent copying – in whatever format that takes!

Think about it

Would you spend hours and hours creating something for somebody else to get the credit for? If so, why?

The copyright holder may grant you a **Creative Commons** licence allowing you to use their material. There are a couple of different types of CC licence:

- CC BY – You can use the material however you want as long as you quote the source.
- CC BY NC – You can use the material only for non-commercial purposes so you cannot profit from its use but must still quote the source.

Other licenses and considerations

GNU Free Document Licence (GFDL) – a licence originally used by Wikipedia and others to share content freely. (GNU is a type of free software for constructing web pages.) Wikipedia now use a CC BY SA (share alike) licence.

If something is labelled as being 'public domain' then it is not copyrighted, so you can use it however you like. This applies to content where copyright has lapsed, as copyright only lasts for a certain length of time (see www.copyrightservice.co.uk/copyright/p10_duration for a concise guide).

However, just because something is found on the internet, it does not mean that it has a public domain status or that it is free to use.

Intellectual property (IP) – this is a piece of work, idea or an invention, which may then be protected by copyright, trademark or patent. The concept of copyrighting an idea is increasingly becoming a bigger issue with the internet.

Certification and classification

Different countries have laws on what is allowed to be seen and shown.

There are several factors that affect the classification with regard to age ratings:
- violence
- strong language
- scenes of a sexual nature.

Certification and **classification** are covered differently depending on the type of media product. The two that you should know about are:
- BBFC (British Board of Film Classification) ratings for film. These ratings are U, PG, 12, 12A, 15 and 18.
- PEGI (Pan European Game Information) ratings for computer games. These ratings are 3, 7, 12, 16 and 18.

Data protection

Figure 2.11 The concept of data protection

Royalty free means that the work can be used without the need to pay royalties (i.e. a fee) each time. However, the work will still be copyrighted. Note that 'royalty free' is very different to 'copyright free'.

Creative Commons (CC) A licence agreement the creator chooses that lets you use that person's copyrighted resources.

Check your understanding

Briefly explain the difference between copyright free and royalty free.

Hint: One of these may still require you to pay a fee per use.

Certification is the process of informing the audience broadly on the suitability of content. It is an important consideration when thinking about the target audience.

Censorship is when artists/filmmakers are not allowed to show their complete work.

Check your understanding

You see a DVD box for sale in a shop window. It has a PEGI logo 7. What sort of product is it?

Data protection is covered by legislation under the Data Protection Act 1998 although several amendments have been made since. There are eight principles but the main points are:

- The Data Protection Act is a series of UK laws designed to protect individuals and their personal data.
- Organisations cannot collect and keep your personal information without following this law.
- Everyone has right to view and correct their own personal information that is held by an organisation.
- Data has to be accurate, for a specific purpose, used fairly and stored securely.
- Data can only be held for a reasonable period of time.
- Data cannot be passed to other countries without adequate protection.

Failure to follow these rules can result in an investigation by the Information Commissioner's Office (ICO) and potentially a fine for the organisation.

Other legal issues

Figure 2.12 Disputes may be settled in court

People have the right to privacy and it should not be invaded. This needs to be considered at all times in the pre-production and production stages of a project.

Defamation, slander and libel are offences under English law. You can't say or write nasty or untrue things about someone without proof. If you say something incorrect, it can be slander and if put in writing it can be libel. You must be careful how you portray people, including what you say and write about them at all times of pre-production and production.

Exam tip

Avoid making any reference to something being copyright free just because you are using it in an educational context – the examiner wants to know if you understand the implications of copyright in a commercial context. This is the same in any unit for the qualification.

1 Fill in the table with what you might find in client requirements.

Information	Defined by client requirements?
Deadline for delivery	
Colour scheme	
Budget	
Salaries	
Target audience	
Mind map	
Storyline	
List of equipment needed	

2 An activity on a work plan is made up from a series of tasks. True or False?
3 A production schedule is needed for any project. True or False?
4 What is the difference between project duration and project deadlines?
5 Complete the following table with examples for each category of a target audience

Target audience category	Examples
Age	
Gender	
Ethnicity	
Location	

6 What legislation restricts an organisation storing information about its customers?
7 Any images found on the internet are copyright free. True or False?

Exam practice

Music Snackbox magazine have provided the following scenario/brief.

Music Snackbox will launch the first edition of the magazine in February and there will be a printed version each week on a Thursday. The digital version of the magazine will be updated daily by 11.00 a.m. The front cover of the magazine will always contain an image of an artist who has released a new recording that week or performed live, across the middle of the page. On the right of the page there will be the titles of three articles from inside the magazine. The magazine will include a rating system for each new release using icons like stars.

1 (a) Identify **three** client requirements other than the Thursday publishing date for the printed version of the magazine. [3]

(b) The printed version of the magazine will be published on a Thursday. This will require that it is printed during Wednesday afternoon and night.

  (i) The project will require the creation of a weekly work plan for each printed issue of the magazine. Explain one effect that this time constraint will have on a work plan for the magazine. [3]

  (ii) Identify **three** items that the magazine work plan would include. [3]

  (iii) Identify **one** type of software that could be used to create a work plan and describe how it could be used for this task. [3]

2 The target audience for *Music Snackbox* can be classified using different categories.
For each of the categories listed explain, using examples, how it could be applied to the magazine.
• Gender   • Ethnicity   • Location [6]

3 What could you use to digitise a hand-drawn mind map? [1]

4 The magazine will include photographs that have been taken by photographers other than those working for the magazine.
Describe one step that *Music Snackbox* magazine would have to take to allow them to use these photographs. [2]

CHECKED ☐

LO3 Be able to produce pre-production documents

Creating pre-production documents

In this section, you will create one or more of the four different types of pre-production document and analyse a short script to identify key information. You will also have to demonstrate your knowledge of file formats and their properties for different types of media product. Keep in mind that at least one of the exam questions will ask you to create some form of pre-production document, which may have a significant number of marks. Let's review the key skills that you will need.

Creating a mood board

REVISED

In section LO1, we reviewed the content of a mood board. In the exam, you will only be able to create the concept of a hand-drawn mood board, although you will need to know about other ways to create one as well.

Key points

- There is no set structure so the content can be placed at random.
- The content does not have to be copyright free – the use of a mood board is there to show similar products and ideas which can help the generation of ideas.
- A mood board is not placed in the public domain – it is for personal or 'in-house' use only.
- The content should have some relevance or connection to your own project, brief or scenario.

Creating a mood board by hand

The content is likely to need a range of images. These can be placed on the mood board or redrawn. Annotate the mood board with notes and comments to show what you are thinking.

Figure 3.1 A physical mood board

> **Check your understanding**
>
> What would be the purpose of a mood board if the project is about creating an advertisement?
>
> *Hint: Think about who is going to use it and why.*

> **Exam tip**
>
> Check to see what the marks are given for in any question that asks you to create something. For example, it might refer to content, layout and fitness for purpose. Annotations are always a good idea to show you clearly understand what is required.

Remember that unlike a visualisation diagram, there is no set structure to the mood board. The content can be placed at random but the important thing is that it follows a theme which is suitable for the client requirements.

Creating a mind map/spider diagram

In section LO1, we reviewed the purpose, structure and content of a mind map.

In the exam, you will only be able to create a hand-drawn mind map although you will need to know other ways to create and digitise them.

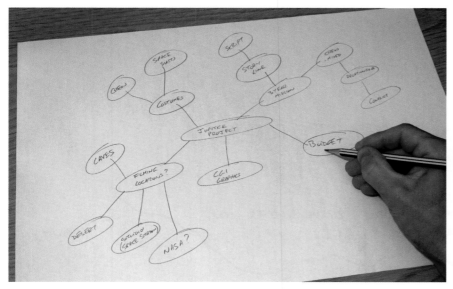

Figure 3.2 A hand-drawn mind map

> **Check your understanding**
>
> How could you use a mind map for a client that needs a new website?
>
> *Hint: Think about the range of pages and content for each one.*

Key points

- There is no set structure so the content can be placed anywhere on the page/sheet.
- The content *must* be linked by connections and have some sort of logical *flow* or breakdown.

Creating a mind map by hand

The content will need to include a wide range of relevant ideas using a clear structure of nodes and sub-nodes that are connected by lines. Annotate the mind map with notes, comments and extra ideas.

> **Exam tip**
>
> Make sure all of the content that you put on the mind map is relevant to the question.

Creating a visualisation diagram

In section LO1, we reviewed the purpose and content of a visualisation diagram.

In the exam, you will only be able to create a hand-drawn visualisation diagram although you will need to know about other ways to create and digitise one.

Key points

- The visualisation diagram should illustrate what the intended final product will look like.
- The content should be relevant to the brief, show where different elements will be positioned and identify what colours could be used.

Creating a visualisation diagram by hand

The content is likely to need a range of images, graphics and text. Annotations are always a good idea to show you clearly understand what content is required.

Figure 3.3 A visualisation diagram annotated with comments

Creating a storyboard

In section LO1, we reviewed the content of a storyboard. In the exam you will only be able to create a hand-drawn storyboard although you will need to know about other ways to create and digitise them.

Key points

- The storyboard needs to show the flow of the story or sequence so that the viewer can get a good 'feel' or impression of what the final product will look like.
- Scenes should show the visual content and be supported by information such as camera shots, action and expected duration.

Creating a storyboard by hand

The content will need a range of visual images for each panel or scene. Annotate the storyboard panels with descriptions, shot types, camera movement, timings, speech, action/direction and any other comments.

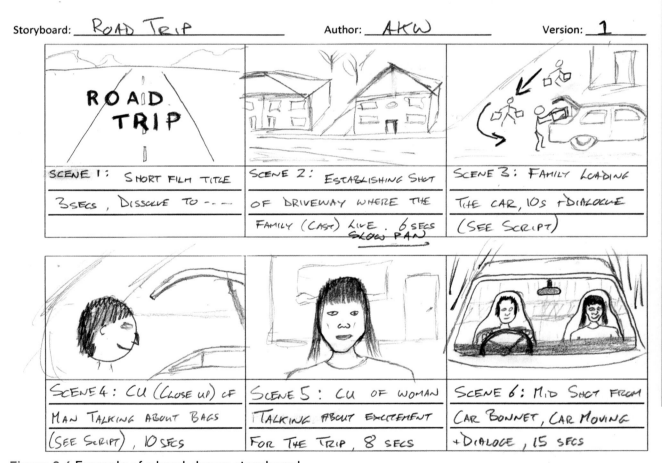

Storyboard: ROAD TRIP   Author: AKW   Version: 1

SCENE 1: SHORT FILM TITLE 3 SECS, DISSOLVE TO ---

SCENE 2: ESTABLISHING SHOT OF DRIVEWAY WHERE THE FAMILY (CAST) LIVE. 6 SECS SLOW PAN

SCENE 3: FAMILY LOADING THE CAR, 10S + DIALOGUE (SEE SCRIPT)

SCENE 4: CU (CLOSE UP) OF MAN TALKING ABOUT BAGS (SEE SCRIPT), 10 SECS

SCENE 5: CU OF WOMAN TALKING ABOUT EXCITEMENT FOR THE TRIP, 8 SECS

SCENE 6: MID SHOT FROM CAR BONNET, CAR MOVING + DIALOGUE, 15 SECS

Figure 3.4 Example of a hand-drawn storyboard

Check your understanding

What would be the purpose of a storyboard for an animated advertisement?

Hint: Consider both the client and the production team.

In section LO1, we reviewed the structure and content of a script. In the exam, you will only be asked to analyse a section of a script and not create one.

Key points

- There is a set structure to a script so the key information should always be in the same place and style. The structure defines the formatting and layout of the script content.
- By analysing the script, you should be able to identify where the action takes place, what happens in the scene, who features in the scene and what they say.

> **Think about it**
>
> Which is more likely to be created first – a storyboard or a script? Give a reason for your answer.

> **Check your understanding**
>
> What information would be in a script but not in a storyboard?

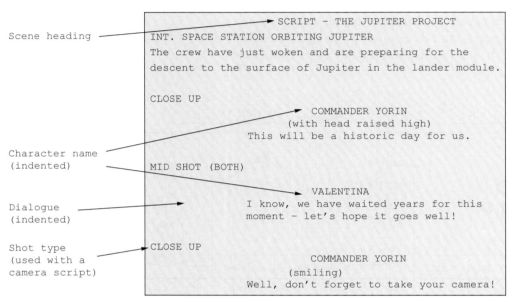

Scene heading

Character name (indented)

Dialogue (indented)

Shot type (used with a camera script)

```
                              SCRIPT - THE JUPITER PROJECT
INT. SPACE STATION ORBITING JUPITER
The crew have just woken and are preparing for the
descent to the surface of Jupiter in the lander module.

CLOSE UP
                        COMMANDER YORIN
                      (with head raised high)
                  This will be a historic day for us.

MID SHOT (BOTH)

                          VALENTINA
          I know, we have waited years for this
          moment - let's hope it goes well!

CLOSE UP
                          COMMANDER YORIN
                           (smiling)
          Well, don't forget to take your camera!
```

Figure 3.5 Example of a formatted script

Note that the different sections are indented from the left-hand margin (but not centrally spaced). At the left-hand side, information is provided about the scene location, action and any camera shots. Indented from this is the character/actor name and what they say (i.e. their speech). By adding detail to the speech, such as how and when they say it, we call this dialogue.

These are the main sections in the script and they should follow some conventions in the way they are formatted. When analysing a script, a standard layout makes it easier and quicker to find the information that you need.

> **Check your understanding**
>
> The names of characters in a video advertisement may appear in which two important pre-production documents?

File formats for pre-production documents

The file format will be typically determined by the software used to create the document, for example:

- word processed documents – .doc, .docx or exported as .pdf
- image files – .jpg, .png, .psd or exported as .pdf.

The general rule would be to save the pre-production files in the standard format for the software being used and then export them in a format that can be viewed on a different computer system that may not have any specialised software.

File formats for final media products

These will be determined by the client requirements, intended platform and what type of media product is being created.

Figure 3.6 File formats for documents

Image file formats

Figure 3.7 File formats for saving still images in Adobe Photoshop

Table 3.1 File formats for still or static images, i.e. images that do not have any movement

File format	Properties and use	Limitations
jpg	Provides lossy compression to reduce the file size at the expense of image quality. Widely used with digital cameras and websites.	Reduced image quality with higher compression settings.
png	Provides lossy compression and supports transparency. Intended for web use as an alternative to .gif files.	Not as widely supported (or popular) as jpg.
tiff	Very high quality lossless image files. Used in high quality printing but losing popularity.	Very large file sizes, which restricts transfer and distribution.
pdf	An export format from image editing software which cannot be edited further. Used with documents and print products with image content.	Cannot be edited directly – must use the original file format before being exported.
gif	Provides small file sizes and supports transparency and animation. Used in website pages for web buttons, logos and other basic graphics.	Limited range of colours and has licensing restrictions since the format is protected by copyright.

Audio file formats

Table 3.2 File formats for audio files

File format	Properties	Limitations
mp3	Compressed file format that can be compressed using different bit rates, providing a range of options for the sound quality and file size. Good for portable devices and widely supported.	Audio quality can be a limitation when using high compression in order to obtain small file sizes.
wav	Uncompressed high quality audio files intended for Windows® computers.	File sizes can be large.
aiff	Uncompressed high quality audio files and the default for Apple Mac® computers.	Cross platform restrictions, not always widely supported.
ogg vorbis	Similar to mp3 but less widely used.	Not widely supported.

Moving image file formats

This includes both video and animation products.

Video file formats

Table 3.3 File formats for video files

File format	Properties	Limitations
mpg	Video file format with lossy compression that provides smaller file sizes for faster loading.	Compression can lower the video quality.
mp4	A video compression standard that enables high quality video over low-bandwidth connections.	
mov	Widely used for video files from digital cameras, providing good quality. Originally developed for use with Apple QuickTime®.	
avi	Uncompressed video file format for high quality. Often used when editing video before exporting in other formats.	File sizes can be very large.
flv	Flash video file, providing smaller file sizes. May be used with both video and animation products.	Not as widely supported.

Animation file formats

Table 3.4 File formats for animation files

File format	Properties
swf	Compressed file formats provide small file sizes for fast loading speed online but not well supported by Apple® platforms.
gif	Limited colour support but useful for short animations that are supported by web browsers.
flv	As for video file format.
mov	As for video file format.

Compression

In general, this is a way to make files smaller. There are two types.

Lossless – This is where no information is discarded or thrown away when saving the file. It retains all of the original information and quality but file sizes are higher.

Lossy – This can have multiple levels and uses algorithms to discard some of the original information in order to reduce the size of the file. This is useful for web use or to minimise the required storage capacity but at the expense of quality. A smaller file is faster to upload, download and share online.

Check your understanding

Complete the table with two different file types for each of the media products shown.

Media product	File type and extension	File type and extension
Music event poster for printing		
Graphical image for multimedia/web use		
Video teaser trailer for a short film		
Video advert for web use		
Animation		
Scenic photograph for printing		
Product photograph for use on a website		
Radio jingle		
Comic book for web distribution		

File naming conventions

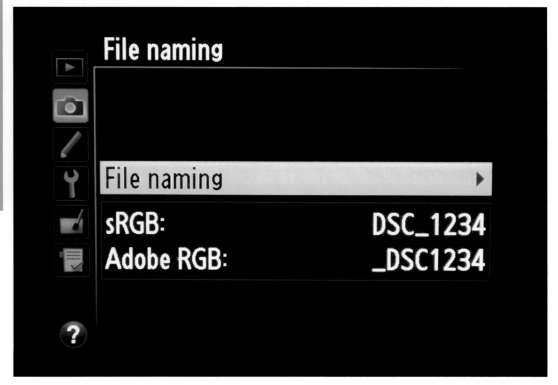

Figure 3.8 File naming on a digital camera

Original filenames created from digital devices are usually in a number sequence. For example, a digital camera might use _DSC2048.jpg but when selecting images for a portfolio it is a good idea to rename files so they have relevant names. This might include a person's name (for a portrait) or a location, event name or date.

Naming conventions also apply to any documents and files that you create. It is always a good idea to set a naming convention for pre-production documents. If creating a new file, the default name might be something like _untitled-1.psd or _document1.doc but a more descriptive name should be used when saving or exporting the file so that others know what it is before opening it. In addition to a descriptive name for the file it is good practice to keep track of the different versions.

Version control

Whenever changes are made as a result of improvements, a new file name should be created. This can include a difference reference at the end to show the latest version such as 'V_0.1' which is edited to become 'V_0.2', for example:
- Advert_storyboard_V_0.1 and Advert_storyboard_V_0.2

Instead of a version numbering system, another option is to use a date code to show when it was created, for example:
- Comic_script_15-08-2015.docx and Comic_script_21-09-2015.docx

Think about it

If you produced a mind map for a project six months ago and it was called mind_map.jpg – how would you know what project it was for?

Figure 3.9 Do you know what version it is?

Exam tip

Questions are likely to check your knowledge and understanding of which file types are suitable for what purpose. So for an image file, it might depend on how and where the image or graphic is to be used (for example, not all image file formats are suitable for the web).

Check your understanding

Think of some filenames for the pre-production documents in the table below. Make them a mixture of files with descriptive names and others that have version control.

Document type (all digitised)	Example filename
Mood board for new superhero comic book	
Mind map for music festival website	
Visualisation for music CD cover	
Storyboard for film trailer	

Which would be the latest version in each of the following pairs of files?

Filename	Tick the latest version
Script v_1.2	
Script v_2.1	
Film_trailer_innovation_24-11-2016	
Film_trailer_innovation_30-09-2016	

Now test yourself

TESTED ☐

1 Create a mood board for the music magazine.
2 Create a mind map of the options for the content of the digital magazine.
3 Snackbox wants to produce a promotional video for the magazine. Create a storyboard with six panels for the content. Make sure that you include an introductory title, scenes with the magazine content and closing information about the weekly publishing.

Exam practice

A music publishing organisation Snackbox have provided the following brief.

Music Snackbox will launch the first edition of a new magazine in February and there will be a printed version each week on a Thursday. The digital version of the magazine will be updated daily by 11 a.m. The front screen of the digital magazine will always contain an image of an artist who has released a new recording that week or performed live, across the middle of the page. There will also be a set of images related to the main articles inside that can be clicked on to navigate to the articles. The front screen will also contain other information and must be easy to use to navigate through the digital version of the magazine.

1 Create a visualisation diagram of the front screen for the digital version of the *Music Snackbox* magazine.
  Marks will be awarded for
  • content
  • layout
  • fitness for purpose
  • annotations to justify your decisions.   [7]

2 (a) Identify **one** suitable file format for the digital version of the *Music Snackbox* magazine.   [1]
  (b) Both the digital and printed versions of the magazine will contain images.
    (i) Identify **one** image file format that is suitable for use in the digital version of the magazine.   [1]
    (ii) The same images will also be saved using the TIFF image file format for use in the printed version of the magazine.
      Explain why the TIFF file format has been chosen for this use.   [2]
    (iii) One of the images used in the magazine has been saved using the following file name:
      WingedBeatLarge.tiff.
      Explain how the writers of the magazine know that this image is to be used for the front cover of the printed version of the magazine.   [2]

CHECKED ☐

How to review pre-production documents and identify areas for improvement

How to review pre-production documents

REVISED

Figure 4.1 Consider all aspects of what has been created

You must be able to review critically any type of pre-production document. This means commenting on its strengths and weaknesses, in addition to how well it meets the requirements of the user. Note that the user of a pre-production document is not usually the final target audience. For example, the person who creates a storyboard for a film might not be the person who will be using it to edit the video footage in the software. Both of those people are still part of the production team, as opposed to the final target audience who will be watching the film at home or in the cinema.

Pre-production documents are used by your client and a media developer, so your comments should be aimed at them or whoever is identified in the exam paper question.

Key areas to cover in a review

- Compare the document back to the brief and client requirements – does it do what was asked for?
- Is the format of the document suitable for the type of media product that is to be developed? For example, a mood board is not going to inform a web developer what to put on the home page.
- Think about the style and whether it is clear for the user of the document.
- Is the content of the document suitable for what the client needs the final media product to do?

> **Think about it**
>
> Who is the audience for the pre-production document? Is it the client or media developer? Write your answer for them.

- Describe the strengths, positives, advantages and benefits.
- Describe the weaknesses, negatives, disadvantages and drawbacks.
- Use technical language and terminology where possible.

How to identify areas for improvement

In addition to reviewing a document, your answer will also need to comment on areas for improvement.

Think about who the pre-production document is for and describe what improvements could be made.

Areas to consider might be the use of colour, content, layout, clarity of story flow, whether everything is covered or if there are significant gaps.

To complete your review, write a conclusion that summarises what you have already put.

Figure 4.2 Consider who is the user of your review. Is it the client or somebody else?

Exam tip

It is likely that a review-based question will also carry some marks for your use of English and credit will be given for your use of spelling, punctuation and grammar. Keep this in mind and write your answer clearly, keeping your sentences well structured.

Now test yourself

Make a list of four things to check for when reviewing a draft pre-production document.

Exam practice

The following storyboard is the first draft of 20-second web advert that will be used to advertise the *Music Snackbox* magazine. The storyboard will be shown to the advert's director.

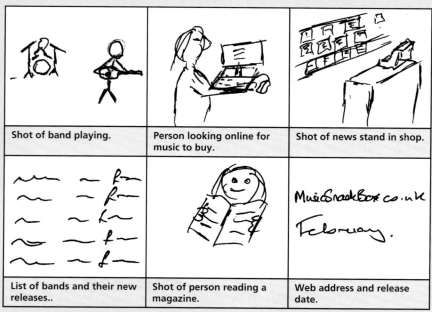

Shot of band playing.	Person looking online for music to buy.	Shot of news stand in shop.
List of bands and their new releases..	Shot of person reading a magazine.	Web address and release date.

1 Discuss the suitability of the storyboard for the advert. You should include any areas for improvement. [12]

Now test yourself answers

LO1

1

Media product:	Mood board	Mind map	Visualisation	Storyboard	Script
Poster for music event	✓	✓	✓		
CD or DVD cover	✓	✓	✓		
2D/3D character	✓	✓	✓		
Comic book	✓	✓	✓	✓	✓
Company Website	✓	✓	✓		
Animated short film	✓	✓		✓	✓
Radio jingle		✓			✓
Video advertisement	✓	✓		✓	✓
Computer game	✓	✓	✓	✓	

2 Storyboard and script although a mind map and mood board could be included.

3 Character names, dialogue (which is a detailed description of what is said and how it is spoken), narration/voiceovers and scene direction.

4 Mood board or mind map.

5 Storyboard and script.

6 Script.

7 Visualisation diagram.

LO2

1

Information	Defined by client requirements?
Deadline for delivery	Yes
Colour scheme	Yes
Budget	Yes
Salaries	No
Target audience	Yes
Mind map	No
Storyline	Maybe
List of equipment needed	No

2 False – a group of related activities is what makes up a task.

3 False – it depends on what sort of project. A video project might use one but not necessarily a graphic design.

4 Duration is how long something will take but a deadline is when it must be completed by. For example, a deadline might be four weeks but a project duration is only two weeks so that there are two weeks spare.

5

Target audience category	Examples
Age	16–18; 18–25; 25–40
Gender	male, female and trans-gender
Ethnicity	British, Indian, Arabian, Eastern, Western, Asian
Location	local, national, international

6 Data protection.

7 False – unless it specifically states that the images are copyright free.

LO4

- Is the content suitable?
- Does it identify any colour scheme and is it needed?
- Does it provide enough information to the user of the document?
- Will it meet the client's requirements?

Exam practice answers

LO1

1 **(a)** Mood board (1)

(b) Two marks for suitable point and expansion, for example:

Allows you to select colours (1) that could be used for the magazine style (1); Can collect ideas (1) from existing magazines (1).

2 Three from:
- Title (1)
- Colours (1)
- Main image (1)
- Price (1)
- Smaller images (1)
- Issue number (1)

LO2

1 **(a)** Three from:
- Daily update at 11.00 a.m. (1)
- Image of artist on front cover (1)
- Image across middle of page (1)
- Three article titles on right side of page (1)
- Icon-based rating system (1)

(b) Three marks for a suitable explanation of effect on timeline, for example:

(i) The Wednesday printing deadline (1) means that the articles all have to be written by end of work on Tuesday (1) so that there is time to set the layout for printing (1).

(ii) Three from:
- Front cover layout milestone (1)
- Main article write-up (1)
- Page layout milestone (1)
- Concert review (1)
- Wednesday lunchtime deadline (1)

(iii) Three marks for suitable software with full description of how it could be used, for example:

Spreadsheet software (1); the cells can be colour coded (1) to show different timescales (1).

Project Management Software (1) will allow tasks to be created (1) that have resources allocated to them (1).

2 Six marks for suitable answers in matching pairs, for example:
- Gender: Parts of the magazine could be targeted at females (1) with a section on boy bands (1).
- Ethnicity: There could be special focus sections on different ethnic music (1) such as MOBO (1).
- Location: The digital version could have regional reviews (1) such as local acts in Cardiff (1).

3 One mark for suitable device:
- Digital camera (1) (NB must refer to 'digital')
- Scanner (1)
- Smartphone camera (1) but not just 'smartphone'

4 Two marks for suitable description of step that would need to be taken, for example:

Must contact photographer (1) and ask for permission to use image (1).

Must acknowledge photographer (1) when image is used in magazine (1).

LO3

1 Visualisation is marked as a whole.

Marks available	Description of criteria	Areas to cover
Level 3 6–7 marks	Visualisation diagram is fully appropriate for front screen of a music magazine. Annotations fully justify decisions made.	Visualisation diagram shows understanding of the use of: layout and white space; appropriate colour scheme; appropriate content for magazine front screen. Annotations fully justify appropriate details on visualisation diagram.
Level 2 4–5 marks	Visualisation diagram is mostly appropriate although some elements will be missing or not used correctly. Annotations may be weak.	
Level 1 0–3 marks	Visualisation diagram will be weak in structure and content will not be fully appropriate. There may be no justifications.	

2 (a) One mark for suitable file type:
  - PDF (1)
  - SWF (1)

(b) (i) One mark for suitable image file format:
  - PNG (1)
  - JPEG (1)
  - SVG (1)

(ii) Two marks for suitable explanation of use of TIFF file, for example:

TIFF files hold high resolution images (1) which are better for use on printed versions of the magazine (1).

(iii) Two marks for a suitable explanation, for example:

The file name contains the name of the band (1) and the large size of the image that will be need for the front cover (1).

The filename contains the large size (1) for the front cover and its file type is a TIFF which is used for printed versions (1).

LO4

1 Marks are applied once the whole answer is read.

Marks available	Description of criteria
Level 3 9–12 marks	An excellent understanding of the effectiveness of the storyboard and its usability by the advert's director is expressed. Reference is made to the degree of content included and how effective this makes the storyboard for the advert's director. The strengths and weaknesses of the storyboard are covered with improvements being suggested and justified against the storyboard's use. Subject-specific terminology will be used correctly and there will be few, if any, errors in spelling and punctuation.
Level 2 5–8 marks	A good understanding of the use of the storyboard is expressed. The strengths and weaknesses of the storyboard are covered although they may be one-sided. There will be some suggested improvements but these may not be wholly suitable and not fully justified. There may be errors in spelling, punctuation and grammar which may not be intrusive on the meaning of the work.
Level 1 1–4 marks	A limited understanding of the use of the storyboard will be expressed. Strengths or weaknesses will be addressed but these may only be in a list of points. Few if any improvements will be suggested and those that are will not be justified. There will be errors in spelling, punctuation and grammar that may affect the meaning of the work.

Introduction to Unit R082 Creating digital graphics

This chapter is all about digital graphics for unit R082, which is needed for the achievement of any Creative iMedia qualification. In this you will learn about the purposes, properties and planning of digital graphics together with the tools and techniques needed to create them.

In general terms, the content of this digital graphics unit (like all the others) is split into four parts. These are:

● Investigation/exploration of digital graphics
● Planning the creation of a new digital graphic
● Creating a digital graphic and exporting for different uses
● Reviewing your digital graphic.

Completing your final assignment

Once you have learned all the required parts of the unit, you will complete an assignment that will be used to assess your knowledge and skills of the subject. It will be set in a vocational context, which means that it will simulate what it would be like to be given a project by a client or employer in a work situation.

You will use the OCR assignment or a modified version of it for the assessment. This assignment will include a series of tasks that follows the same process and sequence of the unit, to explore, plan, create and review a digital graphic.

Task 1: You will be asked to research and explore the purposes and uses of digital graphics. This should be in a broad range of areas that are not restricted to the assignment scenario.

Task 2: You will be asked to plan the development of your work. This means developing your own personal interpretation of the client brief and then considering what assets will be needed, how long it will take and what your intended graphic will look like.

Task 3: You will be asked to create the digital graphic that you have planned. This should demonstrate a variety of skills using a range of tools and techniques in your chosen image-editing software application. You will then need to save/export your graphic in two different formats, one for print and one for web use, which will have very different properties.

Task 4: You should review your final work. This means thinking about things like overall quality, fitness for purpose and any areas for improvement. It is not just a summary of how you created the work – it should be a reflection by yourself on how suitable it is for use by the client in the scenario described in the brief.

With the production of any creative media project, before starting to create it, it is important to think about what you need to produce and what the final work should look like. Since this is a vocational qualification and the assignment is in a vocational context, it will be important to check the suitability of what you have produced before submitting it to the client.

The development of these skills will be a great benefit when you are asked to produce something in the real/commercial world of employment.

Introduction to digital graphics

Digital graphics are used in a very wide range of areas for different purposes. Just because they are created as a digital file doesn't mean that they are only used in digital formats since many print products such as magazines and posters are created digitally using image-editing software. The market is enormous for new digital graphics every day. Throughout this unit you will learn about not just how and where digital graphics are used but also the process and techniques of creating them.

Figure 5.1 Digital graphics are being used on these advertising boards in London

LO1 Understand the purpose and properties of digital graphics

Why digital graphics are used

To answer the question 'why are digital graphics used?' we have to think about their purpose, which is a concept that you may already have studied in the pre-production unit R081. The purpose and type of product are closely linked. For example, for an advertisement in a magazine the purpose is to promote sales of the product that is being advertised. On the other hand, for a comic strip the purpose is to entertain the reader. The main purposes of digital graphics are as follows:

- To entertain: Examples are comics and any still graphics that are used in games.
- To advertise: This is a very large market for graphics and found in many formats such as magazines, newspapers, vehicles and posters in addition to their use on websites.
- To promote: Closely related to advertisements but can be broader in scope, e.g. to promote healthy eating such as the five-a-day campaign. Typically connected to other purposes such as to advertise, inform or educate.
- To inform: Examples are posters, leaflets and instructions, such as those created for health advice or how to use something.
- To educate: Closely related to informing but with a clear objective, e.g. the achievement of a qualification or anything that aids learning.

How digital graphics are used

Some areas where graphics are used are:

- Print publishing (magazines, leaflets, newspapers, books, posters)
- Advertising (print and digital graphic file formats)
- Websites (banners, navigation buttons and image-based content)
- Presentations (title slides and eye-catching graphics to maintain audience interest)
- Games (game box covers and still images used within the game and any promotion of it).

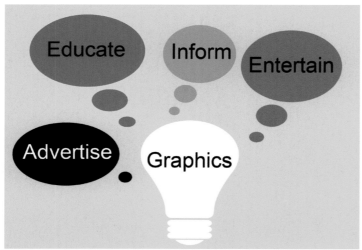

Figure 5.2 Possible uses for digital graphics

Many of these graphics are used in more than one format. So for example, a film could be distributed on DVD and Blu-ray so a front cover is needed that appeals to the target audience. This cover may also be used in a large advertising poster to gain a broader promotion. For use on retail websites and streaming services such as iTunes and Netflix, smaller versions of the graphic with fewer pixels are needed to make sure the webpage loads quickly.

Types of digital graphics

There are two main types of digital graphic which have very different characteristics.

Bitmap/raster images

Bitmap or raster images are based on pixels and are produced by digital cameras or scanners. They are the most common type of file for any graphic that includes pictures. These pixels contain colour information as a mixture of red, green and blue. There is a limit to how far they can be enlarged or viewed at high magnification, because the image will become 'pixelated', that is, the eye can begin to see the individual pixel shape, colour and position. For use on a computer screen, you will need to use either 72 dpi or 96 dpi (dots per inch). For print use, you will ideally need 300 dpi but good results can be obtained from 200 dpi upwards. One of the potential disadvantages of bitmap graphics is that they do not scale well. If you open a bitmap image in an application such as Adobe Photoshop and begin to zoom in to a magnification larger than 100% per cent, you will notice that the image is broken down into small squares (keep zooming in and this will become even more obvious). Each of these little blocks is a pixel that contains only one colour. If you enlarge a bitmap image too far, you will notice that the image quality suffers from 'pixelation' because it is composed of these individual pixels or 'colour squares'.

Vector graphics

The other type of digital graphic is called a vector graphic which is independent of resolution and maintains crisp edges when resized. These do not use pixels and the edges are very smooth even when resized, without any loss of graphical quality. This is because they are based on mathematical formulae that represent curves and lines. Vector graphics are typically shapes and text that are drawn using the shape, pen or text tools. Vector graphics can be converted to raster images for further editing as needed.

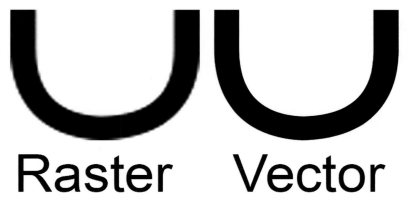

Figure 5.3 Bitmap or raster-based graphics at high magnification

Figure 5.4 Vector-based graphics at high magnification

File formats

The most important image file formats are given in the following table.

.jpg	This is the most common image file format, used in digital cameras and supported by web browsers. It gives a range of options for the amount of compression to reduce the file size, but at the expense of image quality. The format was originally developed by the Joint Photographic Experts group (JPEG).
.png	Portable Network Graphics, an alternative to .jpg but with the benefit of supporting transparency. Intended as a replacement for .gif images without any licensing restrictions. PNG is supported by the World Wide Web consortium.
.gif	Graphic Interchange Format, originally developed by CompuServe. This has a very limited range of 256 different colours, so is more suitable for graphics and logos than photographs. However, it does support animation and transparency. It is commonly used on web pages (e.g. for navigation buttons and other basic graphics) even though officially the patent is still held by CompuServe.
.tiff	Tagged Image File Format is now less popular, partly due to its very large file size. However, it is still sometimes used in print and desktop publishing applications because of its very high quality with no loss of detail.
.eps	Encapsulated PostScript is used within high-quality desktop publishing applications.
.psd	Adobe Photoshop Document – this is the generic format used by Adobe in its graphics software. This format retains all the layers within the file structure for later changes or editing purposes.
.spp	A proprietary file format that is used by Serif Photoplus, which supports image information such as layers in a similar way to Adobe .psd format.
.dpp	A proprietary file format that is used by Serif Drawplus.
.svg	Scalable vector graphics file format, which can be used across different vector graphic editing software applications.
.psp	PaintShop Pro document – this is the generic file format used by Corel in PaintShop software applications.
.pdf	Portable Document Format – this is a widely used format for images, manuals, desktop publishing and other documents that combine text and images. However, a pdf is not an image file format that can be used for editing – it is only exported from the image-editing software for proofing and/or print use.
.bmp	This is a bitmap file format developed by Microsoft for its graphics subsystem. It is usually uncompressed and can support a range of different colour depths.
.wdp or .hdp	A file format used by Windows Media for high-quality photo images with good tonal range. Expected to be replaced with the .hdp file format.

Properties of digital graphics and their suitability for use in creating images

An important part of creating any digital graphic is to make sure that it will be suitable for use, i.e. it is fit for purpose. What the graphic is going to be used for will determine what the image properties will need to be.

The most important image properties are:
- Pixel dimensions: The combination of how many pixels wide by how many pixels high.
- DPI resolution: A property of an image that states how many 'dots per inch' to use. Printing requires typically 300 dpi whereas web use only needs 72 dpi.
- Compression settings: This is connected to the file format, e.g. jpg or tiff and potentially what quality settings have been chosen. The purpose of compression is to reduce the file size but it can be either lossy or lossless compression. As an example, jpg files have different quality settings that affect the final file size. A lower quality setting discards information, which means it will be lossy compression and the image will not look as good when enlarged.

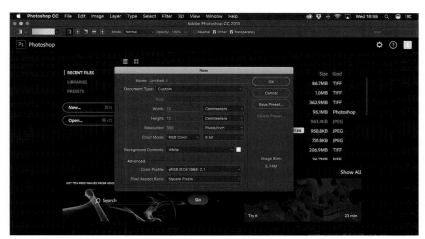

Figure 5.5 Checking the image properties

Other properties can include the colour mode, colour profile and bit depth but these are more advanced features. The most likely colour mode would be RGB although sometimes it might be saved as a CMYK for printing. The colour profile is most likely to be sRGB since this is supported by printers and the web. The alternative is Adobe RGB (1998), which is sometimes selected on a digital camera. If the camera saved the digital photo as a raw file then it might be 16-bit colour depth but jpg would be 8-bit (also the most common). If you haven't changed any of these, they are likely to be an RGB colour mode, with an 8-bit colour depth and sRGB profile.

How different purposes and audiences influence the design and layout of digital graphics

As a learning activity, you could analyse a range of existing graphic design products, which will help you to recognise what would be needed for a specific purpose and target audience in a future product. The important part here is to think about the influence on the design and layout of something that you will create, rather than just review what has been done before. Let's consider a few categories for the design and layout:
- Use of colour: Colours can stimulate different moods in the viewer. Some are warm or cool and others are neutral. Some typical associations of colour are with certain moods so that reds, oranges and yellows are bright, energetic and warming whereas blues, greens and purples can

be settled and cooling. Neutrals can be used for a larger area and then a highlight colour can be used to attract the viewer's attention and give a more targeted message. The genre or theme of the product will also affect the choice of colours. For example, a film aimed at very young children might use bright colours such as blues, pinks and yellows but these wouldn't be suitable for a darker crime theme. An action and adventure poster is probably going to use bright energetic colours to convey that sense of mood to the viewer and target audience.

- Composition: A typical style of digital graphic combines images and text to create the final product. The layout of the combined elements is what we call the composition. Although there are no fixed rules as such, the following are a few key areas to consider:
  - Positioning of the main object or subject so that there is a focus point for the eye
  - Using lines to draw the viewer's attention to the main focus point, which can be achieved using 'leading lines'
  - Using perspective (similar to using lines)
  - Using balance, e.g. are all the elements symmetrical in the final graphic or is the intention that something stands alone and separate?
  - Using suitable typefaces or fonts, e.g. a science fiction theme probably wouldn't work with an antique style font. This is closely related to consistency of style within the final graphic.
- White space: This is any area within the final graphic that is blank. It is not necessarily the colour white but could be any plain colour. It can be used effectively to separate out the different elements or parts of the graphic.
- Styles: This is related to the genre of the final work. It means that the overall style should be consistent with what would be expected, so for example antique fonts and sepia-toned images would work for historical pieces whereas futuristic or digital style fonts and images of alien worlds could be used with science fiction.

Assignment Practice

Let's explore the use of digital graphics:
1 Collect some images from a range of magazines and advertisements (this can include posters and DVD or Blu-ray covers for films or games).
2 Make a list of what has been used to make up the graphics, e.g. multiple photographs (how many?) and text (where is it placed, how big?).
3 State what you would expect the pixel dimensions and dpi resolution to be for all of the graphics (base your estimates on 300 dpi for print use and measure the graphics with a ruler).
4 What is the general style and who is the graphic aimed at (e.g. crime, thriller, action/adventure, science fiction etc. and who is the typical target audience)?
5 List some key features or reasons why you think the graphic is good (or not, as the case may be).

CHECKED ☐

Try the following questions to check your knowledge and understanding of the use of digital graphics.

1　Identify three different purposes of digital graphics.
2　Identify three possible export file formats for print use (i.e. not specific to the image-editing software).
3　Identify one file format that would be used on the web but not for print.
4　If a graphic is 200–300 dpi, what is its most likely use?
5　If you are to design the front cover of a box for a car-racing game, what colours might you choose?
6　If you are to design a large A1-size poster to advertise clothes for a fashion store, what properties would be needed for the main images that would be the full size of the poster?
7　You have downloaded an image from the internet, to be used for a film poster which is to be a print product at 30" × 20" (inches). However, the image properties indicate that it is only 842 × 595 pixels and 72 dpi. Why is this?
8　For the film poster in question 7 – what would you expect the properties to be for the print product?

L01 Understand the purpose and properties of digital graphics

LO2 Be able to plan the creation of a digital graphic

Interpreting client requirements

Before starting any work on creating a digital graphic you must review what is actually required by the client. This will be stated in their client brief. You might have some good ideas about what you have always wanted to produce but if these don't meet the client's needs then it has no practical use, and in a commercial world you may not be paid or have the opportunity for further work.

Let's start by looking at the client brief or specification. Read this document carefully and think about how to satisfy the needs of the client using your own creative talents and ideas. Note down some ideas on the content and layout (or composition) of what could work. You could discuss your ideas with the client before starting any work, which is a typical approach within the graphics industry.

Using your knowledge from R081 pre-production, you could summarise the following key points:
- State what media product is needed
- State the purpose of that media product
- Identify who the target audience will be
- List ideas for the content of the media product
- Identify timescales for when the product will be needed
- Identify any constraints and restrictions
- State the details of any house style to make sure the product is consistent with the organisation's own branding and recognised style.

It is quite likely that the initial set of client requirements in their specification will not answer everything. This is where you might need to request further information by one of the following methods:
- Client discussion
- Request a more detailed brief, script or specification.

The client might have some thoughts about what they want but your own ideas on how to achieve that will be the basis of your own interpretation. This expansion and interpretation of the brief is an important first step for you as the graphic designer. A good way to do this is to produce a spider diagram or mind map with your different thoughts and ideas, which then brings in some of your knowledge and skills from pre-production unit R081. Another option if you need some inspiration for ideas is to produce a mood board with images from similar and/or related products.

Understanding the target audience

You could again refer to the content from R081 here so that you can identify and categorise the target audience. The expectations, needs and requirements of the target audience must always be considered so that the media product can be successful and this is much easier when you know how to categorise them. The main areas are:

- **Age**: Be clear about the age group that will be the target audience for the digital graphic. This can be a range such as 6–12, 12–18, 18–40, 40+.
- **Gender**: Typically, male and female but also consider trans-gender.
- **Ethnicity**: We are a multi-cultural society so the effect of the graphics on different ethnic groups should be considered. Ethnic groups can be defined as a group of people that have a common background or culture, whether through race, religion or language.
- **Location**: This can be described as local, national and international. The use of a digital graphic might target one of these groups more than others, such as an advert for a small local music event compared with a poster for a national music festival.

Producing a work plan for graphics creation

This is another aspect of pre-production planning that is included in R081. Note that work plans are also known as project plans but the key points are summarised here.

Contents of a digital graphic work plan

LEARNED ☐

- Tasks – the different stages or main sections of creating the digital graphic
- Activities – a series of things to do in order to complete a task
- Durations – the amount of time that a task or activity is expected to take
- Timescales – how long it will take to complete the graphic
- Milestones – key dates when a section is completed
- Deadlines – a date when something must be completed by
- Contingencies – 'what if' scenarios, back-up plans such as extra time or alternative ways to do things
- Resources – the hardware and software needed to do the tasks and activities. Although part of the overall plan, these may not be shown on the actual work plan.

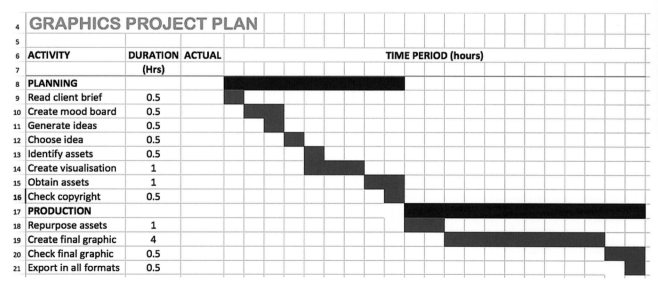

4	**GRAPHICS PROJECT PLAN**					
5						
6	**ACTIVITY**	**DURATION**	**ACTUAL**		**TIME PERIOD (hours)**	
7		**(Hrs)**				
8	**PLANNING**					
9	Read client brief	0.5				
10	Create mood board	0.5				
11	Generate ideas	0.5				
12	Choose idea	0.5				
13	Identify assets	0.5				
14	Create visualisation	1				
15	Obtain assets	1				
16	Check copyright	0.5				
17	**PRODUCTION**					
18	Repurpose assets	1				
19	Create final graphic	4				
20	Check final graphic	0.5				
21	Export in all formats	0.5				

Figure 5.6 Example of a work plan

Producing a visualisation diagram

A visualisation diagram can be produced in one of two ways. Firstly, you could draw a sketch by hand of what you want your final graphic to look like. This could then be annotated with explanations of layout, font choices and colours to help the viewer understand your ideas. The second option is to produce the visualisation digitally, i.e. using a software application. This does not have to be image-editing software and could take simpler approaches by using desktop publishing applications, such as Microsoft Word, Apple Pages or Microsoft Publisher.

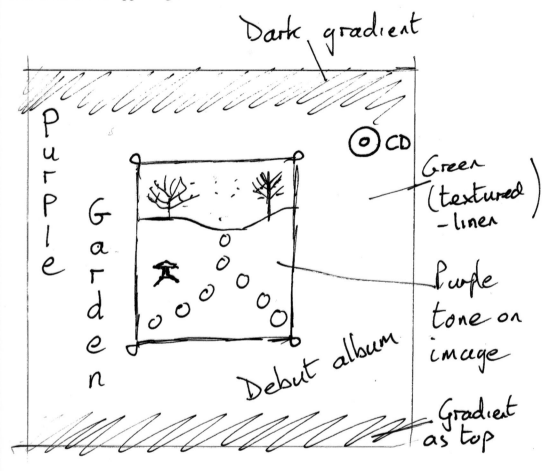

Figure 5.7 Visualisation diagram or sketch

Identifying assets needed to produce a digital graphic

At this stage, the identification of *potential* assets is a planning activity so anything you think of here is only a possibility. The practical sourcing and use of those assets is a separate activity for learning outcome 3 (LO3). However, what you can do here is think about what might work or would be suitable – even if the assets cannot be obtained later. The range of assets could be:

● Photographs: Whether taken by yourself or sourced from the work of others
● Scanned images: These could be taken from any printed material but the copyright implications must be considered

- Library images: These could be from web-based picture libraries or CD/DVDs. Again the copyright or royalty status must be taken into account
- Graphics and logos: These might be supplied by the client in a vocational/commercial context but checks must be made.

A good approach is to make a list of what you might like to use. This could be identified in a table but other approaches can also be suitable. The contents of a table could look something like this:

Image	Source	Copyright status	Potential use

The *image* field should be a descriptive name of the image asset.

The *source* field states where the image is obtained from. Note that 'Google Images' is not a source – it is actually the web page that identifies where the image is located.

Copyright status: Assume it is the website where the image is hosted when working online. Otherwise, it will be clear when using CD/DVDs or scanning from a magazine (in which case the image is most certainly protected by copyright). In this situation, you would need to consider how to obtain permission to use the image.

Potential use: This should be your own thoughts on how you could use the image. Perhaps it will be the main background or just a small image that is placed in a corner? Whatever the use, describe how and why it is suitable.

Identifying resources needed to create a digital graphic

In general, *resources* is a term that covers hardware, software and people. For the purposes of this unit on digital graphics, it is expected that you will be working on your own.

> **Hardware** The equipment to be used such as computer system, peripherals and imaging devices.
>
> **Computer system** e.g. PC, Apple Mac, laptop, desktop, tablet.
>
> **Computer peripherals** e.g. display monitor, keyboard, mouse, track pad, graphics tablet.
>
> **Imaging devices** e.g. digital camera, scanner.
>
> **Software** The image-editing software applications used to create the digital graphics, which does not need to include the software used for writing reports.

Hardware and equipment

LEARNED

The hardware and equipment are physical devices that are used in some way to create a digital graphic. Other equipment can include pens, pencils, paper (since pre-production planning and visualisation documents could be drawn by hand).

Computer system

This could be a PC or Apple Mac (desktop or laptop). Tablets such as an iPad or Android device could be used if suitable apps are available and you can show the process of creating the graphic. If using a PC or Mac, some type of image-editing software would need to be installed (see the later section on software options).

Figure 5.8 A computer system

Digital camera

Figure 5.9 Digital cameras can be used to create original images

When using a digital camera, there are two important key areas to consider:

- What type of image is needed for use with the graphic? For example, which orientation (portrait or landscape) and what should be the main subject of the photograph? These elements are part of the overall photographic composition.
- What features and settings of the digital camera will be needed? For example, it might need a fast shutter speed to freeze a movement or flash if it is quite dark.

If the photograph is blurred or out of focus then it will not be much use and an alternative image will be needed. In general, image editing can only make very limited improvements if there are fundamental problems. However, if the composition is not ideal, you may be able to crop the image in the software to make it more suitable for the layout of the graphic.

Scanner

Scanners typically connect using a USB connection and are used to scan text documents, images and graphics. Typical uses when creating digital graphics are the scanning of logos or images for use on one of the layers in a graphic montage. The process of using a scanner is as follows:

- Place the (printed) document or image face down on the glass plate.
- Slide the document to the corner that is marked with an arrow to identify the origin or starting point of the scan.
- Either use the scanning software provided with the scanner installation, or import the scan directly into the graphics editing software. In Adobe Photoshop, this is typically found from the 'File' menu > 'Import'.

The WIA driver is used for basic scanning although more control can be found using the dedicated driver for the scanner. A scan resolution of 300 dpi is recommended for most graphics although 150–200 dpi can also be suitable in some situations.

Figure 5.10 Using a scanner

Graphics tablet

This is an alternative to the standard computer mouse. The use of a stylus pen on the tablet is similar to using a brush on paper and so has become popular with creative artists and designers. The thickness of a line can be changed by increasing or decreasing the pressure of the stylus on the tablet.

Internet

There is an enormous range of images and graphics on the world wide web. Many of these can be found using an image search but the results do not always show images that would be a suitable resolution for print purposes. The pixel dimensions of the image determine its suitability, so look at the pixel dimensions and divide these by 300 to determine how large they could be (in inches) as part of a print-based product. This is based on a conventional print resolution of 300 dpi. The second restriction on potentially using images from the internet is the copyright status – most images are protected even if that is not clearly stated.

Choosing image-editing software

LEARNED

The following is a list of software applications that can be used to create and edit your digital graphics.

- Adobe Photoshop: A widely used industry standard application used with photographs and graphic design. The professional-level versions are part of the Adobe Creative Suite but lower-cost alternatives include the Elements versions that are aimed at the home user.
- Adobe Illustrator: Also an industry standard for professional use, but more specific to graphics design and the use of vector graphics.
- Adobe Fireworks: This was originally produced by Macromedia and popular with those using graphics within web development and animation work. However, this was taken over by Adobe and is being phased out.
- Serif PhotoPlus: This is a good option for creating digital graphics and is accepted as image-editing software. A wide range of tools is available that could be used to create digital graphics.
- Serif DrawPlus: A powerful software application although slightly more suited to desktop publishing than image editing. Serif PhotoPlus would be a better choice for this unit.
- Serif Affinity Photo and Designer: The professional-level version was designed for use on Apple Mac but a Windows version is now available.
- Corel PaintShop Pro: An alternative to Adobe software that supports both bitmap and vector graphics.
- Pixelmator: A dedicated image-editing software application for Apple Mac. You can edit photos, sketch, draw and paint, add text and shapes, and then apply enhancement effects in a similar way to other advanced image-editing software.
- Gimp: A freely distributed open source program for photo retouching and graphical image creation.

Some other applications can be used to edit graphics but not all of these would be appropriate. Some examples would be Microsoft Publisher, Word, PowerPoint, iPhoto and Paint. Many of these are Microsoft Office-based applications that are more suitable for desktop publishing rather than graphics image editing.

Legislation in digital graphics production

You will need to document any use of copyrighted, trademarked or intellectual property when creating your digital graphics. As part of this you should keep records of all sources and permissions obtained for any material that is not your own. You may also need model and/or property releases for people and property that may be identified in your work. These releases are used to show that you have the right permissions to use the photographs in your final digital graphic.

Copyright This is a legal right that allows the owner to distribute, licence and profit from its use, which is typically for a limited period of time. In the UK, that usually means 70 years after the author's death. Once the copyright has expired, it changes its status to 'public domain', which means it can be freely used by anyone. Note that the copyright owner is not always the original author or creator since copyright can be transferred.

Trademarks These are used to identify an organisation or product and their use is protected by law. The general rule is that these should not be displayed in a graphic without permission from the trademark holder. Logos are a typical example.

Intellectual property If you have created something then you will own the intellectual property unless it was produced as part of an employment contract. Copyright and trademarks are two forms of protecting intellectual property but other forms include patents and documented designs.

Royalty free This means that the work can be used without the need to pay royalties in the form of a fee each time. However, the work is most likely to be copyrighted. Note that royalty free is different to copyright free.

You should also refer to the information in the chapter on R081 pre-production which explains more about the legal issues of copyright and legislation. For the purposes of digital graphics, 'published' material is usually protected by copyright and includes:

- Photographs
- Images and graphics
- Content of books and magazines
- Still images from films
- Content on the internet.

To use published resources, you must check the licensing restrictions. Even if there are none shown:

1 Contact the owner.
2 Ask for permission to use it.
3 Be prepared to pay a fee.
4 Obtain written permission to use the image.

Some people are happy for their products and work to be used by others but still want to have some protection and recognition. In the UK, copyright does not have to be registered – it is automatic and belongs to the author or creator unless transferred by written agreement. Remember that you cannot get around copyright by creating your own version of somebody else's work, e.g. by tracing around it or photographing it.

Copyright protection is there to prevent copying – in whatever form that takes!

For the purposes of digital graphics, you may need to include the use of certification and classification symbols, such as those from the BBFC and PEGI. Refer to the previous chapter on R081 pre-production for more information on what these are.

Assignment Practice

Here's an example assignment brief:

You have been asked to plan the development of a full-page magazine advertisement for a fashion clothing store. The magazine page size has been set at 8" × 11" so your graphic must be to this size at 300 dpi. A visualisation diagram has already been produced which is in the style of a grid, 4 blocks wide and 5 blocks high.

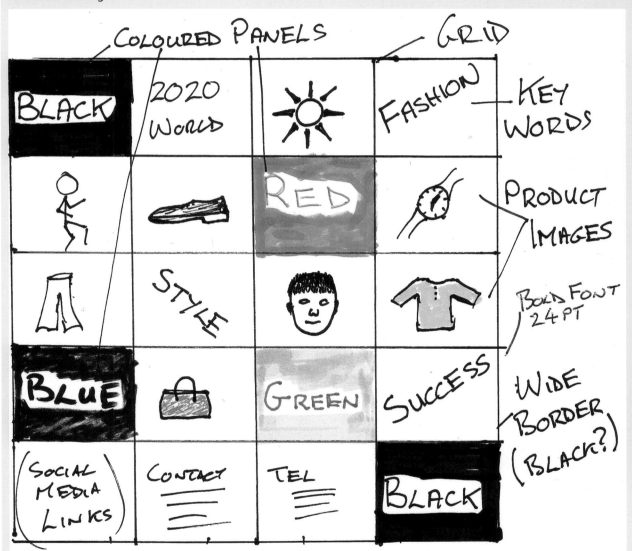

Figure 5.11 Visualisation diagram for the advertisement

At this point, you could now develop your own ideas about how to meet this brief. Start with a spider diagram of ideas and then move on to sketch out some visualisation diagrams of your own. The following questions can be based on the visualisation diagram shown or one of your own.

CHECKED

Now test yourself

Try answering the following questions.
1 What questions might you have for the client?
2 Identify what assets would be needed to create the advertisement.
3 Identify what resources will be needed.
4 Categorise the expected target audience for the advertisement (age/gender/ethnicity/location).
5 What legal issues will you need to consider when creating the advertisement?
6 Draft a work plan that includes a range of activities, from obtaining the assets to producing the final graphic.

Activity	Duration	Timescale			

7 Finally, on a separate piece of paper, try sketching your own ideas for alternative layouts and designs for the advertisement. You could use inspiration from your practice exercises in LO1 where you looked for a range of graphic advertisements.

L03 Be able to create a digital graphic

This is where you apply all of your planning by creating what you have visualised. There is a sequence of activities to complete for this:

1 Obtain the assets needed, either by sourcing or creating them.
2 Prepare the assets for use in the final graphic and store them in a suitable location.
3 Create the graphic using a range of tools and techniques.
4 Save and export all the required versions for different uses.

Throughout this section we will be exploring the use of a wide range of tools and techniques, which will be applied to a digital graphic project. This will be in the form of a music CD cover for a local band.

Sourcing assets for use in digital graphics

Sources for images and graphics could be:

● Internet: searching the web can locate a wide range of images but there are limitations (see below)
● Client: for their own logos
● Photographers: commission-based work
● Picture libraries: most of these have a website to browse and purchase images
● Picture CD/DVD: sometimes given away free with magazines
● Printed materials: will need to be scanned.

When using the internet, an image search is likely to display many pages of results. One of the limitations is usually the image size in terms of pixel dimensions and dpi resolution. If an image is used on a web page, it only needs to be 72 dpi and no larger than the display monitor. Unfortunately, that tends not to be much use if wanting to use the image in a print product since print resolution needs typically 300 dpi. An advanced search on images can be selected so that only images larger than a specific size are shown in the results. This is a better option to ensure the image assets are going to be technically compatible with what you want to do. However, that brings us on to the second restriction which is the permission for use. Most of the content on the web is protected by copyright and you may need permission from the owner to use it. Try not to use the clause that it is for educational use only since the qualification aims to develop knowledge and understanding of working in a commercial or industry context. If working in the media industry, you would need to know how to obtain copyright clearance and permissions, so this is what you should be demonstrating in your work.

Creating assets for use in digital graphics

The planning of the final graphic may have identified the need for some specific assets that must be created. An example would be a logo, symbol or other graphic that would be part of the finished design. This may have to be drawn digitally in the image-editing software application or created from other assets that were a starting point.

The creation of assets may use many of the same tools and techniques as those used to create the final graphic. Therefore, many of these have been included in the later section of this chapter.

Ensuring the technical compatibility of assets

This is an important consideration when creating any digital graphic. The technical properties of an image asset include the pixel dimensions and dpi resolution. Since you will be creating a print product, you will need to be using assets that can be printed with 300 dpi at the intended size. Therefore, if you had sourced an image from the web at 600 pixels wide and 72 dpi, it would only be any good if printed at 2 inches (50 mm) maximum width. If this was the image that you wanted to use as the background for an A4-sized page, it would not be technically compatible. If that is the print size that you want then for an image to be technically compatible it would have to be around 2500 pixels wide and/or 3500 pixels high. However, it is possible to edit image assets and crop or resize them to make sure they are technically compatible. Let's have a look at that process next:

1 Open the image asset in your image-editing software.
2 Check the image properties. In this example it is a 6-megapixel photo (3000 × 2000 pixels).
3 The intended use is for the background image of the music CD cover, which we have identified in the planning as being 12 cm square (or 4.724 inches). That means 4.724 × 300 dpi = 1417 pixels vertically and horizontally.
4 The pixel dimensions of the image are greater than what we need, which is good since we cannot create detail that doesn't already exist. Because it is larger than what we need, it will be technically compatible.
5 To edit this asset for use, we just need to crop the section that we want at a size of 12 cm square with 300 dpi. Use the crop tool in the image-editing software and set the properties for the final asset in the options bar before using it.

Using image-editing software

The options for suitable types of image-editing software applications were reviewed in the resources section of LO2. One of these should be used to initially edit, create and save/store the assets for use in the final graphic. Once these assets, or component parts of the graphic have been created, work can then start on what will be the final product. A good approach in this unit is to collect together all of the assets into one folder including logos, copy text and a range of images that will be used for both the background and foreground graphics.

Some of these assets will need to be repurposed to make sure they are technically compatible (refer to previous section). This will be part of your image-editing workflow and affect the choice of file format and resolution.

Your digital workflow and image processing of assets

The basic editing techniques in most of the available software applications are very similar so that skills learned in one application can often be quickly transferred into something else. One of the aims is to learn a basic workflow, which can be thought of as a standard sequence of editing techniques for every image and graphic. You can then use this workflow in whatever software application you have available in future.

An example of a basic workflow would be:
1 Check the image quality.
2 Adjust the brightness/contrast or 'levels'. (Note that you only need to do *one* of these.)
3 Check and adjust the colour if necessary.
4 Crop to the required size, shape and resolution (this depends on the intended use).
5 Save the image in a suitable format and filename.

Let's look at the techniques and processes for each of these five basic steps and apply them to a range of assets that we have sourced.

Step 1. Check the image quality

This is the first step of any digital graphics workflow when considering the use of an asset (i.e. an image). Basically, if the image quality is not good enough for what you need, you want to know immediately, otherwise you could be wasting your time with further editing. The best way to review the image quality is to use the zoom control to view the image at 100% magnification. Look closely to see whether it is blurred or out of focus on the important subject areas. If the image quality is poor, close the file, open a different image or source/create some alternative images. Remember that you cannot put quality or detail back into an image by using a series of editing techniques. You will be able to rescue a poor photograph or image to some extent, but the results will be limited. A much better approach is to start with something good and move on from there.

Figure 5.12 Checking the image quality at 100%

Step 2. Adjusting the brightness/contrast or 'levels'

One of the important and basic techniques as part of a workflow is to optimise the brightness and contrast. This makes sure that the full tonal range is used in the image, which means the darkest (shadow) areas are true black and the brightest (highlight) areas are true white. Without this optimisation, an image can look either 'washed out' or very dark.

To modify this, you could use the brightness/contrast adjustment sliders, which is accepted as a standard tool/technique. If wanting to do this in a more advanced way, you could use the 'Levels' adjustment histogram manually (i.e. not in automatic mode). However, the first thing to do is make sure you have a reasonable size of the whole image on the screen. You can do this by selecting the 'View' menu and then 'fit on screen'.

The brightness/contrast sliders are a basic tool that allows you to make manual changes visually on the screen. Move the sliders to the left or right until the best-looking result is achieved.

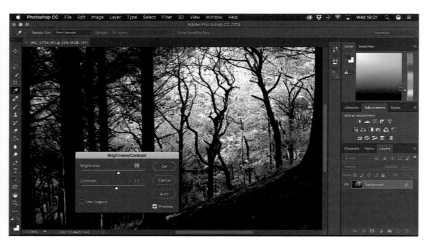

Figure 5.13 Using the brightness/contrast sliders

An alternative standard tool is the 'Auto Levels' function in Adobe Photoshop. The software analyses the content of the image and balances out the range of colours and brightness levels. If the result does not work effectively, you may have to undo this and choose a different way to make the adjustment. A more advanced technique is to adjust the levels manually.

The benefit of making adjustments using Levels is that it displays a histogram of how the image is made up in terms of the brightest and darkest points together with everything in between. The darker levels are shown at the left-hand side and brighter levels at the right-hand side. To make adjustments for the levels, do the following:

- Move the black point slider inwards from the left until it is at a point where the black shading on the histogram just begins.
- Move the white point slider from the right to where the histogram just ends.
- Move the mid-point (gamma slider) to a position that makes the image look the best in terms of the overall brightness and contrast on the screen.

When using the Levels adjustment, note the optimum positions for the black and white point sliders in the image as shown.

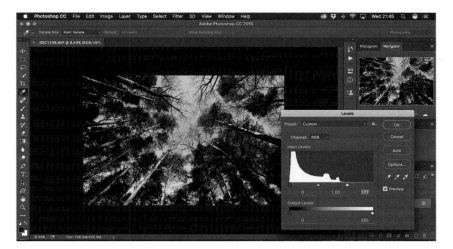

Figure 5.14 Levels adjustment

Step 3. Check and adjust the colour

In Adobe Photoshop Creative Suite (or Cloud) there are a number of options for adjusting the colour. Some of these are:

- Image menu – auto colour
- Image menu – adjustments – hue/saturation
- Image menu – adjustments – colour balance.

The auto colour option may not work well with every type of image, depending on what range of colours is included. The hue and saturation adjustments are a set of sliders similar to the brightness and contrast. They enable you to change overall colour tone and colour saturation. You can also reduce the colour saturation to zero, which removes all the colour to leave a black and white image.

Figure 5.15 Colour adjustment

Step 4. Cropping the image

To crop and/or straighten any image is also a basic image-processing technique. Reasons for the image not being straight could be either a scanned image that was not square on the scanner or a photo from a digital camera where the horizon is not straight across the frame. If wanting to use only part of an image as an asset in a graphic, you may want to crop this from the full picture. Another reason for cropping is to obtain the size and shape that you need. In the example of a CD cover, a square image is needed for the background which is 12 cm × 12 cm. This could be cropped from the middle section of a photograph. To crop and straighten an image in the same process:

1 Select the 'Crop' tool from the Toolbox. If wanting a specific size, this can be entered in the option bar fields as shown. In Figure 5.16 we have chosen 12 cm width, 12 cm height and 300 dpi.

2 Draw a box around the area that is approximately how you want your composition to look.

3 Adjust the position of the corners and edges as needed. Everything that is outside this crop window will be removed when you complete the crop command.

4 To rotate the crop window, position the mouse cursor just outside a corner of the box so that a 'rotate' icon is displayed for the mouse cursor. You can then freely rotate the box left or right as needed.

5 Press 'Enter' to perform the final crop or click on the tick mark in the Options bar.

Figure 5.16 Cropping an image

Step 5. Saving images and graphics

This is where you can save your edited image and graphical assets onto your computer hard disk or other external location. It is a good idea to save a full-size high-resolution image as your master file together with a smaller file (lower-resolution image with fewer pixels) for use at the intended size on the final digital graphic. If you have added any layers to the image asset, then the default will most likely be an Adobe .psd file. This means that it will have to be opened and used in Photoshop later. The jpg file format does not support layers so you would need to 'Save as' or 'Save a copy' if you want to use this widely supported format later. Check that the pixel dimensions and dpi resolution are suitable for your intended purpose because once pixels or image quality are discarded, they cannot be recovered.

To save the image asset – from the 'File' menu, click on 'Save As'. Refer to the section on file formats earlier in this chapter, depending on what the image asset will be used for.

If you were only saving an image for use on a web page, the pixel dimensions are likely to be less than 1200 pixels wide and the resolution should be set to 72 dpi. When saving for print use, the pixel dimensions will need to be high enough for the printed size at a resolution of 300 dpi. So, for example, if the image asset was to be used at 2 inches wide, then it would need 2 × 300 dpi = 600 pixels width as a minimum.

Figure 5.17 Checking the image size and properties

Different image-editing software

LEARNED

The screen layout of different applications varies but the four basic sections are:

1 Workspace/editing window
2 Menus
3 Toolbars with shortcut icons
4 Tools panel.

The basic processes and concepts of creating digital graphics are the same whichever software is being used. These are:

1 Obtain and store the image assets in a working folder.
2 Open the image assets and check the image quality.
3 Adjust brightness/contrast or levels.
4 Adjust/correct colours.
5 Complete any additional editing that is needed.
6 Save with a descriptive filename in a high-quality format.
7 Create the final digital graphic to the required print dimensions by combining the image assets and editing as needed.
8 Save the final graphics with the high-resolution pixel dimensions and resolution required.
9 Resize the digital graphic for web or multimedia use as required by the brief. Save this version as a *separate* file – do not overwrite your high-resolution master file.

Using tools and techniques to create assets and graphics

The first step in creating a graphic is to setup a new image file. The important part here is to make sure the image properties meet what is needed by the client brief (or your own criteria if creating an asset). So, if you are creating an A4 poster for print purposes, it will need to be the following:

● Print dimensions: 297 mm × 210 mm or approximately 11.69" × 8.27"
● Resolution for print: 300 dpi.

Therefore, the pixel dimensions for A4 will need to be 3508 × 2480 based on 25.4 mm per inch. You might need to check what units your image-editing software is using to confirm this. It will be either imperial (inches) or metric (millimetres and centimetres). A quick conversion of

300 dpi is 118 pixels/cm. If you are creating an asset at this stage, you will need to think about what print size the asset will be and this will inform your choice of pixel dimensions. Copy and complete the following table with examples of products that need specific image properties.

Product	Print dimensions (size)	Pixel dimensions
CD front cover	12 cm × 12 cm or 4.724" × 4.724"	
A1 poster	841 × 594 mm or 33.1" × 23.4"	
Magazine advert (approx. ¼ page)	4" wide × 5.5" high	
Blu-ray (front cover only)	126 mm wide × 148 mm high	

Drawing and painting tools

When creating an image asset from scratch, the following tools can be very useful.

Shapes: These are created as vector-based graphics and so they are scalable for any size or resolution. There is a library of shapes built into all versions of Adobe Photoshop in several categories.

Pencil: The pencil tool allows you to draw thin lines or change the colour of individual pixels, which is similar to using a very narrow brush. You would often use this at 100% or higher zoom.

Brush: The brush can be used with quick masks and for freehand painting or filling in shapes. There are different sizes but always larger than the pencil.

Eraser: This is used to permanently erase parts of an image that is not wanted. Note that the eraser is considered to be a standard (basic) tool so you might want to consider using selection tools instead of just erasing a background. The use of selection tools is covered later in this chapter.

Gradient: This is best created on a new layer to allow editing and further modification. A gradient will consist of two defined colours, which are foreground and background. When editing images, changing the foreground colour to transparent can be one of the most useful types of gradient since this creates a very natural blending effect. Alternatively, when creating original graphics from a blank worksheet, a two-colour gradient can provide more dynamic visual effects than plain colours. These gradients can have a linear (straight line) or radial (circular) change.

Figure 5.18 Using a gradient

Changing the foreground/background colours: At the bottom of the Toolbox can be found the foreground and background colour boxes. Click inside each box to display the colour picker window to choose a new colour. The default colours (black/white) can be set by clicking the smaller icon at the side. The colours can be exchanged by clicking the two-way arrow.

Using and applying filters

There is a large range of filters and effects available in Adobe Photoshop. Some of the more popular examples are:

- Distort
- Liquefy
- Artistic (Watercolour, Paint daubs)
- Blur.

Filter effects can be applied to individual assets, such as background images or smaller image assets that have been placed on top of the background image. Try not to rely too much on filters though, since it is easy to ruin a graphic that is basically sound.

Figure 5.19 Some of the filters available in Adobe Photoshop

Adding text

Most digital graphics will include some sort of text in the form of a title or information.

Figure 5.20 Adding text to a graphic

An example of this can be found in the practice exercise to create the logo for the music CD cover later in this section.

General purpose tools and techniques

Undo is a common feature of all software applications and reverses what you have just done. Adobe Photoshop CS has a much more powerful and flexible history palette. This allows you to go back in time to a specific point that can be seen in a table of actions.

Changing image or canvas size

You should always keep a high-resolution image as your master file since this can always be repurposed for use at a lower resolution. However, if the detail and quality is not there in the first place, you cannot create it later. Using the high-resolution master file, you can change the image size or crop it to the required dimensions and resolution needed by the client or project. A low-resolution version is also much easier to send by email for proofing purposes. You can check or modify the image size and resize it from the 'Image' menu – 'Resize' – 'Image size'. A box appears as shown:

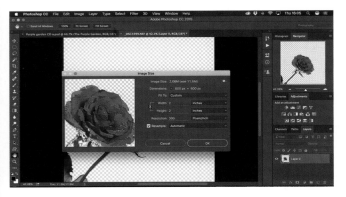

Figure 5.21 Image size box

This shows the number of pixels in the image and the printed document size for a given resolution (i.e. number of pixels per inch). You can change the number of pixels, print size or resolution so that is suitable for other uses. Each of the field boxes are linked and changing one field will have an effect on the others at the same time. Make sure all the settings are as you need before clicking on 'OK'.

Check your understanding

Now let's try the following exercises to create a logo and asset for use on our CD cover.

Step 1: Insert a shape. In this example we have chosen a dog paw print to represent the 'Dog paw' record label. Draw the shape at the required size using the mouse to 'click and drag'.

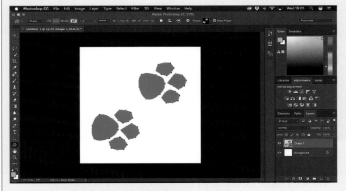

Figure 5.22 Inserting a shape

Step 2: Fill the shape with a chosen colour. You can use the colour picker to set the foreground colour and then the 'fill' or 'paint bucket' tool. Click once inside the box to change it. The colour for the shape can be set before drawing it using the options bar but you can also change it afterwards.

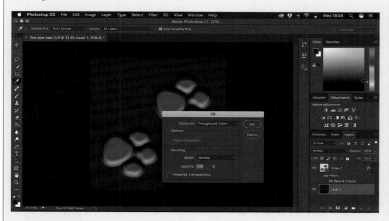

Figure 5.23 Fill with a different colour

Step 3: Layer styles – bevel and emboss. These are typically used to add a 3-dimensional effect to a shape or object. Drop shadows produce a straightforward 3D effect but here we want to create some texture to the surface of the shape as well.

Figure 5.24 Adding a layer style – bevel and emboss

Step 4: Delete the background layer (by double clicking on the name and renaming to Layer 0, which unlocks the layer for editing – then delete).

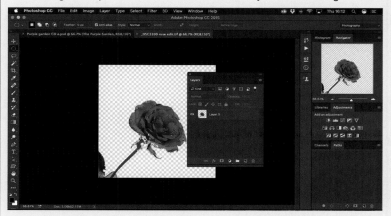

Figure 5.25 Deleting the background layer to make it transparent

Placing the assets and creating the digital graphic

LEARNED

The techniques and processes involved in creating the digital graphic are best practised by following an example, which uses a range of commonly used tools. You can work through some graphic projects later in this chapter but the basic steps are:

1 Create the new image file (see previous section on how to create a new image file with appropriate properties).
2 Import the assets to be used. These can be opened and then copied (or dragged) onto a new layer. Note that each asset will be placed on its own new layer.
3 Use the move tool to position and scale the assets as needed.
4 Enhance the visual effects on assets. This could include layer styles, gradients, blending and filters.
5 Add titles and any other text required.

Using more advanced tools and techniques

LEARNED

Before going through the process to create a digital graphic product, let's look at some more of the tools and techniques that could be used. As a starting point, we need to know the difference between standard tools and advanced tools. Of course, some of these could also be used when creating the individual assets and not just the final graphic.

Standard tools	Advanced tools
Brightness/contrast	Levels
Auto levels	Curves
Auto colour	Manipulating layers
Move tool	Layer styles (e.g. on text)
Eraser	Selection tools
Adding text	Feathering
Adding basic shapes	Cloning and healing tools
Applying filters	Gradient effects
	Stroke and fill
	Text special effects
	Modifying shapes with effects
	Burn and dodge

Note that in the following sections, the use of advanced tools is identified using the {**Advanced**} tag.

Using the Curves adjustments {Advanced}

This is a versatile tool that means you can brighten and darken an image together with adding contrast and adjusting the colours. It can be thought of as a more advanced version of the Levels adjustment.

The curves graph displays input and output levels, initially as a straight line. You can modify the image by changing the shape of the line. As an example, you can increase the contrast by changing the shape of the curve to look like an 'S', whereas to decrease the contrast it would be an 'inverted S' shape.

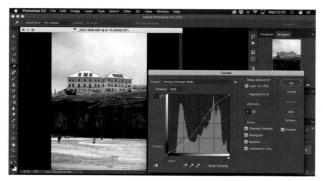

Figure 5.26 Increasing contrast using a curves adjustment

Using and manipulating Layers {Advanced}

The Layers palette shows how an image is constructed and a new digital graphic will have just a single background layer. Each additional layer can be thought of as a sheet of glass which is transparent in the parts that are shown as a checkerboard pattern. You should always imagine that you are looking down on these layers from above, i.e. the top of the layer stack. This is because the top layer is seen first and you will be able to see through all the transparent areas to anything that is underneath.

Individual layers can be added, turned off for editing, renamed or moved. Contents can also be changed and skilful use of layers is a great way to create complex digital montages.

Figure 5.27 A digital graphic made up with multiple layers

Layer styles is covered elsewhere in this chapter – see the practice exercise to create the logo for the music CD cover.

Using Layer styles {Advanced}

These are typically used on text, shapes and sometimes objects that have been cut out and placed on a new layer.

Figure 5.28 Adding a layer style

An example of using this can be found in the practice exercise to create the logo for the music CD cover later in this section.

Using selection tools {Advanced}

Selection tools allow you to define parts of the image so that you can make changes to those parts without affecting the remainder of the image. Another way to use selections is to copy and paste selected parts of an image onto other layers or different image files so that you can assemble a graphic montage. When using selections, an active selection area appears with a flashing dotted line around it, sometimes referred to as 'marching ants'.

The toolbox includes a range of selection tools for use with shapes and colours. Adobe Photoshop also includes smart selections which works well on some parts. Brushes can be used to create or modify selections. You can add or subtract areas to a newly defined selection area using the options toolbar. In Photoshop Creative Suite and Creative Cloud versions, there is also a quick mask mode where you can use the normal brush tool with the foreground/background colours set to black/white but this is quite an advanced technique to master.

Figure 5.29 Marquee selection

The main types of selection tool are as follows:

Marquee: These use either rectangular or elliptical shapes for regular-shaped outlines in the image. If you hold down the keyboard 'Shift' key at the same time, this will enable you to draw a perfect square or circle.

Lasso: There are three different types of lasso tool:
- The freehand lasso tool works like a pencil on the screen – it follows the mouse when you hold the left mouse button down. Releasing the mouse button joins up the start and end points. It is sometimes useful for adding extra parts into a selection that have been missed out.
- The polygonal tool draws straight lines between mouse click points.
- The magnetic lasso tool attempts to trace the outline of an object by automatically recognising the edges. It works best when there is good contrast between the object you want to select and the background. If you make a mistake in the edge, use the delete key to remove the previous anchor points. This is a good selection tool to become familiar with and learn how to use effectively. There are three settings in the options bar to improve the performance of this tool:
  - Edge contrast is the value that a pixel has to differentiate it from its adjacent pixel and be recognised as the edge.

- ○ Width is the number of pixels either side of the pointer used to find the edge.
- ○ Frequency is the distance between the fastening or anchor points.

Magic wand: This selection tool uses colour to recognise which pixels are to be selected. The options bar has a checkbox to control whether these are either contiguous (all joined together) or non-contiguous (anywhere on the image as long as it is within the colour tolerance).

New/add/subtract/intersect (found on the options toolbar): Having created an initial selection, you can add extra areas or remove them using one of these modes. They are available with all selection tools, so, for example, you could use a magnetic wand selection to start with, change to the freehand tool and choose the 'add to selection' to carry on adding extra parts of the image.

Using feathering {Advanced}

By default, selection tools will create hard edges but these tend to look better with some feathering so that they blend more naturally. The amount of feathering will depend on the number of pixels in the object that is to be selected so some experimentation is often required.

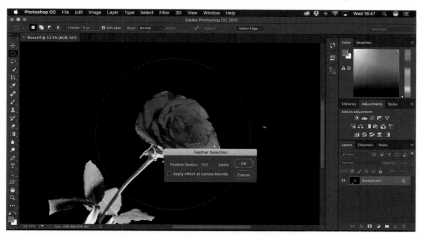

Figure 5.30 Effects of feathering edges

Check your understanding

Creating an image asset that is cut out from a photograph:
1 Open a digital image that has some content that you want to use for an image asset.
2 You will most likely be working on the background layer, which is locked for editing so we first need to remove the protection. To do this, rename the background layer to become 'Layer 0' by double clicking on the name, which then means it can be edited.
3 Use selection tool(s) on the main subject (here we are using an oval marquee).
4 Feather the edges, from the 'Select – Modify – Feather' menu option. Type in a number of pixels to feather across (this needs to be a larger number for high-resolution images, in this example we chose 100 pixels).
5 Invert the selection from the 'Select – Inverse' menu option.
6 Press delete on the keyboard (you should see a chequerboard pattern appearing).
7 Save the edited image with a new filename (do not overwrite the original file).

Figure 5.31 Using the selection tool

Using the cloning tool {Advanced}

The purpose of the clone stamp is to duplicate parts of the image from one section into a different section. This is a very useful tool that can be used to remove unwanted details from an image, although practice is needed to build up your skill level.

To use the clone tool:
- Click on the icon in the tool box once to select it.
- If needed, select the brush style from the 'options' bar although the soft-edged default brush works well on most images.
- Set the required brush size (also in the 'options' bar) by dragging the slider up or down. A useful keyboard shortcut for brush sizes is the left and right square brackets [ ] to decrease and increase size respectively.
- Move the mouse onto the image and position it close to the feature that you want to remove, then press and hold down the 'Alt' key so that the mouse cursor changes to a 'target' icon.
- Single click with the left mouse button, then release the 'Alt' key.
- Carefully move the mouse across the image onto the part to be removed, remembering where you have just clicked for the clone source point.
- Click and hold down the left mouse button so that a cross hair and a circle are shown as mouse cursors. The tool works by copying the colour information from the cross hair (source) and pasting it into the circle (destination). When using this tool, keep an eye on both of these.
- Keep repositioning the source point as needed using 'Alt' click for different parts of the image to be modified and try to avoid repeat patterns.

Figure 5.32 Using the cloning tool

Using healing tools {Advanced}

Adobe Photoshop Creative Suite/Cloud has both healing and patch tools. You can use the healing brushes to remove small blemishes and spots by blending the colours and textures. Having selected a suitable tool size that is typically slightly larger than the blemish, you then just click on it with the mouse.

The patch tool is a large area healing brush and is used by first drawing a shape with the mouse. This area can be used as the 'source' or 'destination' for the blending. This works best when there is a fairly good colour and texture match between the two areas.

Using text and adding effects

Note that the basic use of the type (or text) tool would be a standard tool but this can be enhanced with effects to become more advanced.

Type/Text tool: This allows you to add text to images such as titles and/ or descriptions. Any text is always placed on a new and separate layer so that it can be edited and modified independently. Text is created as vector graphics, meaning that it can be scaled to any size and still maintain a smooth outline. Sometimes these have to be rasterised into pixels to make certain types of changes.

To use the type or text tool, first select the tool from the toolbox and then move the cursor onto the image where you want the text to start. Click the mouse again and type the text that you want using the keyboard. You can also change the font and colour from the 'Options' bar.

Adding text effects: Some adjustments to how the text is displayed can be made using the options bar. The font style, size and colour are the standard options but additional effects can be used to modify the shape. An alternative way to change the look of any text is to add a layer style. A basic drop shadow is a good way to enhance the text using a 3D effect.

Using gradient effects

One way to use this is to place a gradient onto a new layer. To add impact to the image, we have selected the gradient tool with black and transparent as the two colours. You could use two solid colours but this would then need to be lower in the layer stack so that any text or other objects are seen above it. The black to transparent gradient is being used above a background image in the layer stack in the following example.

Figure 5.33 Using the gradient tool

Transformation techniques {Advanced}

This advanced technique allows you to modify the shape or perspective of an image. One example of a use for this technique is to straighten the vertical angles that are seen when photographing tall buildings from low down.

Figure 5.34 Effect of transformation changes

To begin, select the entire image from 'Select' > 'Select all'.

From the 'Edit' menu, click on 'Transform' using one of the options provided.

In addition to using the 'Transform' menu, you can also use 'Ctrl + click' on any of the corners to adjust the individual transformation points.

Additional advanced tools and techniques

Stroke tool: This can be used to create a solid line around the edge of a selection. The thickness of the edge can be set in the tool options.

Fill tool: This can be used to fill a defined area with a specific colour. It is typically used with selection tools to create coloured shapes.

Smudge tool: This is a good way to 'push' colours around. Think of an oil painting when the oils are still wet – you could push the colours around with a finger. This is what the smudge tool does – just click and hold the left mouse button down and push in the direction you want. This tool can be useful when repairing old photographs, although for most of the work in creating digital graphics you are more likely to use the clone stamp.

Blur tool: The blur tool is the opposite of sharpening and effectively blurs the area under the cursor. You can use this for softening edges but anything larger is best done using one of the blur options in the filter menu (such as Gaussian blur which has variable control). If you wanted to soften the edges on an object to be cut out, consider using feathering on the edges before copying the selection as a new object or layer.

Sharpen tool: This does the opposite of blurring, but again is best limited to use on edges. Don't overdo this otherwise you can produce some pretty horrible edges to the subjects of your picture. For larger areas, you can also use the sharpening options in the filter menu (such as the unsharp mask, which has variable control).

Dodge, burn and sponge tools {Advanced}

Dodge tool: The name of this tool comes from a darkroom technique whereby the light is restricted from reaching the photographic paper. This makes the image lighter.

Burn tool: The name of this tool also comes from the darkroom and it is the opposite to the dodge tool. It allows more light to reach the paper, and this makes it darker.

Both the burn and dodge tools are best used on monochrome (black and white images) in small amounts. Try removing the colour from an image and use the burn tool on the highlights at 10–20 per cent. Likewise, try the dodge tool on the shadows with a similar setting of 10–20 per cent.

Sponge tool: This is used to change the colour saturation of selected parts of the image. In Adobe Creative Suite, you can change the mode between saturate and desaturate, depending on whether you want to increase or decrease the intensity of the colour.

Sharpening

LEARNED

Most digital images and graphics will benefit from sharpening before making a final print. The optimum amount of sharpening will depend on the intended use, which is dependent on print size and resolution. It is best not to save a file that has already been sharpened as your master file, as the next time you want to produce a print it may be for a different size and resolution – hence the sharpening values might need to be different and these cannot be undone once saved.

Check your understanding

Creating a graphic for the front cover of a music CD:

Try following these steps in a similar way using some of your own images. With any image-editing software, there are several ways to achieve the same result so if you want to change the process or techniques that is probably fine (but check with your teacher).

1 Create a new image file to the correct dimensions, which is 12 cm × 12 cm at 300 dpi.
2 Open your pre-prepare image assets to be used on the CD cover. Using the mouse, drag each one to the new graphic. Note that each of these appear on a new layer.
3 Place each asset in your chosen position as shown on your visualisation diagram. Some of these may need to be scaled (i.e. made smaller). If so, make sure you don't change the aspect ratio so that they appear squashed either horizontally or vertically.

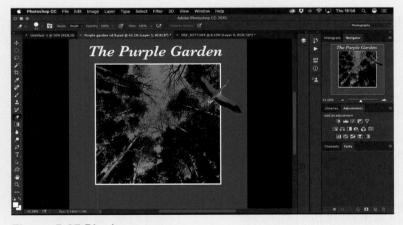

Figure 5.35 Placing assets

4 Blend the edges of the assets as needed, either using gradients, feathered edges or by defining them with a stroke line.

---

5 Add title text and enhance this with a drop shadow layer style to produce a 3-dimensional effect.

6 Add a logo if available (see the earlier exercise on creating one).

7 Save the graphic in its native format (e.g. Adobe Photoshop .psd).

8 Use 'Save as...' to export a copy in a generic format for use by the client (e.g. a jpg or tiff for print purposes).

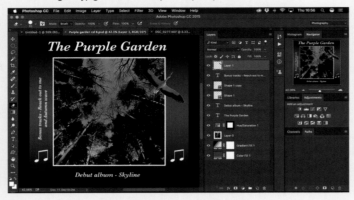

Figure 5.36 Creating the CD cover

Saving and exporting a digital graphic in different formats

This is where you apply your knowledge from LO1 (learning outcome 1) on the different file formats and image properties depending on where the graphic is to be used. As a brief summary, let's first look at the suitability of the different file formats.

File format	Print use	Web/multimedia use
.jpg	Yes	Yes
.png	Maybe	Yes
.gif	No	Maybe
.tiff	Yes	No
.eps	Yes	No
.pdf	Yes	Maybe

Other file formats include .psd, .spp, .dpp, .svg, .psp, .wdp, .hdp. Note that these are all working file formats and final graphics should be exported in one or more of the above.

The second consideration is what the optimum image properties should be for the intended use. The image properties include both the overall pixel dimensions and the dpi resolution.

Print use: Pixel dimensions to be based on print size using 300 dpi. Some examples are shown in the following table. To calculate the pixel dimensions, multiply the print size (in inches) by 300. If you need to convert cm to inches, use 2.54 cm = 1 inch.

Print product	Print size	DPI	Pixel dimensions
CD cover	12 cm × 12 cm	300	1417 × 1417
A4 page	29.7 cm × 21.0 cm	300	3508 × 2480
A3 page	42 cm × 29.7 cm	300	4960 × 3508

Web or multimedia use: Pixel dimensions to be based on a conventional dpi resolution of 72 but the total pixel dimensions are also important to make sure the graphic fits the page and can be downloaded quickly. Unlike print products, there are no calculations as such for this – the pixel dimensions and dpi should be specified in the client requirements. Just make sure the height and width are the right way round.

Using version control

This is also covered in the first chapter on R081, pre-production. You should always use suitable filenames so as an example, _untitled-1.psd would not be good. The aim of using a descriptive file name is so that both you and other people should have a good idea what the graphic is before opening it.

Whenever new versions are created following some changes to the graphic, a new file name should be created. This can include a reference to identify what version it is such as 'V_0.1' which is edited to become 'V_0.2'.

Using the example of the CD cover for our band, we could use something like the following for the two files for print and web use:
a PurpleGarden_CD_Print_Ver_0.3.tiff
b PurpleGarden_CD_Web_Ver_0.3.png

To check your understanding, which of these two should be the larger file size?

Whatever system you choose for file naming, make sure it is easy to identify the product, its intended use and what version it is.

Assignment practice

In this task you will be asked to actually produce or create your work. Some examples would be:
- A Blu-ray cover that includes front, back and spine
- A music CD (with separate files for front and back covers)
- A magazine advert (various sizes between ¼ and a full page)

- The front cover for a magazine
- A poster to promote a film or event.

Pick one or more of these and work through the creation process to practice your skills in using tools and techniques of the image-editing software. Don't forget to draft a visualisation diagram first so that you have an idea of what you want to create before you start!

CHECKED ☐

TESTED ☐

Now test yourself

1 Identify three sources for assets that could be used in a digital graphic.
2 Identify the most important properties of an image that determine whether it will be technically compatible for a graphic that is to be printed.
3 List the five steps for a basic digital imaging workflow.
4 What is the meaning of a grey/white chequerboard pattern on the background of an image asset?
5 Identify three tools or techniques to cut-out a main subject from a photograph.
6 What tool/technique could you use to add a 3D (three-dimensional) effect to a text title?
7 You have created a low-resolution version of a graphic and now need a version for print purposes, which you decide can be created by resampling from 72 dpi to a higher 300 dpi resolution. Is this a good approach?
8 Your client has suggested a gif file for the web version of your graphic but it includes photographic images. Why is a gif file unsuitable on this occasion?
9 You have created the third version of a high-resolution digital graphic for a Blu-ray box cover. What filenames would you choose for a print version and a web version?

LO4 Be able to review a digital graphic

How to review a digital graphic

The concept of reviewing your work is found in all of the units and some additional guidance can be found in the chapter on R081 pre-production. In this unit on digital graphics, you must be able to critically review both the print and web based graphic files. This means commenting on the strengths and weaknesses in addition to how well it meets the requirements of the client. Note that this should be a review based on your own thoughts and analysis of what you have produced rather than stating what other people think. The aim is that you learn how to critically review your own work.

Key areas to cover in a review

LEARNED ☐

- Compare it back to the brief and client's requirements – does it do what was asked for?
- Is the format of the digital graphic suitable? As an example, a graphic for use on a web page is not going to be suitable as a .tiff file.
- Is the content of the digital graphic suitable for what the client needs? So, if promoting a film – are the images consistent with the film, its genre and storyline?
- Is the image content quality suitable in terms of brightness, contrast, sharpness, colour and composition?
- Is the editing of the graphics effective and pleasing to look at?
- Does the final work demonstrate a conventional or creative/innovative approach? There is no right or wrong here – just recognise what has been produced.
- Think about and describe the strengths, positives, advantages and benefits.
- Think about and describe the weaknesses, negatives, disadvantages and drawbacks.
- Use technical language and terminology where possible.

How to identify areas for improvement and further development

Having looked carefully at what you have produced, this should provide you with ideas on how and where the graphic could be improved. Let's look at a few common examples of what these might be:

Size: Does the size or shape of the graphic need changing? Consider both versions (print and web use).

Blurred or unsharp: Do you need to use higher resolution images or change them for something else?

Text not readable: What would improve the readability, e.g. font size or colour?

Poor layout: Could the different assets and elements be repositioned so that it looks better, e.g. is anything too close to an edge or out of balance?

Colour (and contrast): Would you choose different colours that don't clash or do they need to be more bright and vivid?

Further development can be linked to areas for improvement but it may also be how the graphic could be used in additional ways. Some examples would be:

Use in different formats: You may have produced a music CD cover for the case and a web version but what about an advertisement in a magazine for the new CD album? Think about where else the graphic could be used to promote the product.

Enhanced versions: Perhaps the target audience reaction to the graphic was disappointing so it may be necessary to create a new version that has more impact.

Now test yourself

TESTED

In order to test your knowledge of how to review a digital graphic, work through the following practice exercise.

You should now review the final graphic for the CD covers as shown.

Figure 5.37 **Finished CD covers**

Review each of the examples provided. This means thinking about things like overall quality, fitness for purpose and any areas for improvement. When reviewing your own work, it should not be just a summary of how you created the graphic. The type of review that is needed for this qualification should be a reflection by yourself on how suitable it is for use by the client described in the brief and whether the properties, content and layout make it fit for purpose. Identify some of the following key points:

- Size
- Layout
- Use of colour
- Use of white space
- Strengths
- Weaknesses
- Areas for improvement.

Now test yourself answers

LO1

1 (i)   To entertain
  (ii) To advertise
  (iii) To educate or inform
2 Note that some others could also be suitable.
  (i)   tiff
  (ii) jpg
  (iii) pdf
3 gif
4 Print
5 Examples may include red, black, orange etc.
  Just be sure to have thought about the audience
  that might buy your car-racing game, and what
  colours they might want to see on the box.
6 Very high resolution, ideally 300 dpi but more
  than 200 dpi. The pixel dimensions would be
  7016 × 9933 at 300 dpi.
7 It has been exported as a low-resolution image
  for web use so that the page loads quickly. Note
  that 842 × 595 is A4 print dimensions at 72 dpi.
8 Around 9000 × 6000 pixels using 300 dpi
  (30" × 300 = 9000 and 20" × 300 = 6000)

LO2

1 (i)   What sort of content would they like to be
        included in the grid?
  (ii) When is it needed by?
  (iii) Is there a standard logo or colour scheme for
        the organisation?
2 (i)   Photographs of the products
  (ii) Contact information (for text panels)
  (iii) A copy of the organisation's logo (or if one is
        to be created)
3 (i)   Computer system with display, keyboard and
        mouse
  (ii) Digital camera or scanner to capture image assets
  (iii) Image editing software application
4 (i)   Age: Most likely teenage/young fashion 16–25
  (ii) Gender: Male and female
  (iii) Ethnicity: All ethnic groups to be covered so
        images should include multi-racial people
  (iv) Location: UK national market (to cover shops
        and online sales)
5 (i)   Copyright on all image assets to be used
  (ii) Model releases for photographs that show people
  (iii) Advertising Standards Authority regulations

6

Activity	Duration	Timescale					
Create a mood board	30 mins						
Create a mind map of ideas	20 mins						
Draft layout – visualisation	30 mins						
Identify assets to be used	30 mins						
Check legal issues	20 mins						
Obtain assets	30 mins						
Create the advert	3 hours						
Save/export in required formats	20 mins						

7

Product	Print dimensions (size)	Pixel dimensions
CD front cover	12 cm × 12 cm or 4.724" × 4.724"	1417 × 1417
A1 poster	841 × 594 mm or 33.1" × 23.4"	9933 × 7016
Magazine advert (approx. ¼ page)	4" wide × 5.5" high	1200 × 1650
Blu-ray (front cover only)	126 mm wide × 148 mm high	1488 × 1748

LO3

1 (i) Stock image or picture libraries
  (ii) Internet (using an image search)
  (iii) Client
2 (i) Pixel dimensions and dpi resolution
  (ii) File format (i.e. whether it supports a wide range of colours)
3 (i) Check the image quality
  (ii) Adjust brightness/contrast
  (iii) Adjust colour
  (iv) Crop the image as needed
  (v) Save in a suitable format
4 It is transparent.
5 (i) Selection tools, e.g. marquee, lasso, magic wand
  (ii) Crop tool
  (iii) Eraser
6 Layer style
7 No, because the extra detail cannot be created.
8 It doesn't support enough colours for photographic image quality.
9 Examples could include:
  (i) Blu-ray_cover_print_V3
  (ii) Blu-ray_cover_web_V3

LO4

Size

(a) Is a square shape and appears to be suitable dimensions.
(b) Is also a square shape and at suitable dimensions.

Layout

(a) Quite basic, text a bit small and no reason to have the rose image at the bottom, which looks out of place. No name for the CD.

(b) Clean and easy to read, eye catching use of images.

Use of colour

(a) Colour matches the name but does not look very good.
(b) Colours complement each other and good contrast with the text.

Use of white space

(a) Very little white space since background image covers the whole area although the dark gradient at the top effectively makes the text stand out.
(b) The purple gradient around the edges is good and emphasises the image and text content very effectively.

Strengths

(a) The background image has some appeal and a reasonable composition. The text is clean and readable.
(b) Bold use of colour, eye-catching main image that fits the CD album title. The text is very clear and readable with good contrast.

Weaknesses

(a) Use of colour is poor, lacks text information, rose image at the bottom looks wrong and out of place.
(b) Text at the left-hand side is quite small and the use of music notes uncertain. The bird image at the top right could be a bit clearer.

Areas for improvement

(a) Better use of colour, change the image assets (delete the rose), add the CD album title.
(b) Increase the size of font slightly at the left-hand side and edit or replace the bird image at the top right.